L. F.

*The Church in the
World of Radio-Television*

The Church
in the World of
Radio-Television

by
John W. Bachman

ASSOCIATION   PRESS
NEW   YORK

to

Charles and John
of the first generation growing up
in the world of radio-television

Foreword

This provocative but balanced study by John W. Bachman is the outgrowth of converging streams of concern for the relation of radio and television to religion.

It draws first of all upon Professor Bachman's own conviction and his extensive experience in American broadcasting as both practitioner and teacher. He has brought to his subject a technical competence, a sensitivity to the basic human and religious issues, a fairness of mind, and a clarity of expression which will commend the book to all who are interested in the impact of the mass media upon our culture.

The study results also from a growing concern on the part of the public, including many alert Christian laymen, for a larger sense of social responsibility in the radio and television industry. This concern was reflected in the invitation extended to Mr. Bachman by Association Press, the publishing house of a lay organization, the Young Men's Christian Associations, to write a book in this field. This lay concern has been strongly represented in the shaping of the study.

A third contributing stream is the increasing attention being directed by responsible leaders in the broadcasting industry itself to the problem of molding creatively and ethically the tremendous potential influence of the mass media upon the minds and spirits of our people. Industry representatives have been generous in their co-operation with the study. Industry self-appraisals, notably in the field of communications research, have been liberally drawn upon. One authoritative summary of the structure of the television enterprise is included as Appendix A of the book.

The fourth and precipitating ingredient which led to this book has been a series of direct initiatives by the churches. Many churchmen and official church bodies have given voice to the growing recognition in their communions that the mass media hold incalculable possibilities, supportive or obstructive, for the proclamation of the Christian gospel. There is a widespread openness in the churches to enlightened leadership by competent people, not only on the direct use of the media for religious broadcasting but on the total role of the media in the shaping of our culture and our standards of value.

The National Council of the Churches of Christ in the United States of America, on behalf of the thirty-two Protestant and Eastern Orthodox communions which it comprises, appointed in February, 1958, a Study Commission on the Role of Radio, Television, and Films in Religion. The membership of the Commission is listed in

Appendix B of this book. Under the chairmanship of President Wilbour E. Saunders of Colgate-Rochester Theological Seminary, the Study Commission has considered with great care and expert advice over a two-year period a wide range of issues germane to its assignment.

Much of the thinking of the Study Commission is reflected in this volume. As an active member of the Commission, Professor Bachman has taken the Commission's deliberations into account in the shaping of his book, while retaining full freedom and authority as author. The study is not, therefore, an official statement of the Study Commission or of the National Council of Churches. It is an outgrowth of the Study Commission's work and is highly commended by the Commission for its illumination of most of the issues in the field of radio and television with which the Commission has dealt.

It is expected that policy recommendations, consonant with the approach to the subject found in this book, will be made by the Study Commission to the General Board of the National Council of Churches looking toward official actions by the General Board. Beyond the field of radio and television, the Study Commission also is developing recommendations for General Board consideration in regard to films and the film industry.

The National Council of Churches' Study Commission on the Role of Radio, Television, and Films in Religion extends its deep thanks to John W. Bachman and to Association Press for this distinguished book.

> R. H. EDWIN ESPY
> Secretary to the Study Commission
> Associate General Secretary,
> National Council of Churches

Preface

Radio and television are playing so influential a role in modern society that the church has a basic responsibility in relation to the media, a responsibility which, for the most part, has not been accepted or even recognized.

There will be some readers of this book who, seeing its title, will wonder why the church is meddling again in affairs which should be left to others. The venture will appear even more dubious to them if they glance through the following pages and note that we are dealing not only with religious broadcasts but with advertisements, news, and entertainment, and even with the organization and regulation of the American system of broadcasting. Such persons probably will not read the book because its contents will appear to be located too far out on the fringes of the church's task, but they are precisely the ones from whom we should like most to receive a hearing, so that they might better understand the problems.

There are professing Christians who contend that the church has no concern with anything in this world except to renounce and denounce it, but it is difficult to see how such a position can be held by anyone who believes that God has taken sufficient interest in the world to create it and to send his Son into it. The contrasting position which holds that the church has no concern with anything beyond this world is at least as false in the light of the Cross. There is still no more apt description of the Christian situation than "in the world but not of the world," and this applies to modern society as permeated by the mass media, the world of radio-television.

We are in that world. Our lives and our children's lives are being influenced by the mass media. But we also have a loyalty and an orientation which should point beyond that world and thereby give us a sense of direction for living soberly within it. We should be able to enjoy and appreciate its benefits, to transform some of its evils, and to resist much of what we are unable to transform. The church as the community of believers can share ideas and insights which will provide guidance for individuals and families. The church can also impart light and salt through Christian broadcasts.

This task of the church in the world of radio-television will be extremely difficult, and I make no attempt to make it sound easy. The following chapters articulate many perplexing issues. Whenever possible I suggest policies and approaches to meet them. At the end, however, it may appear that I have unearthed more questions than answers, a charge to which I must plead guilty but ask for leniency on the grounds that this is the only honest course to take.

For years in religious broadcasting we have been giving overconfident answers to superficial questions. Now we must ask some fundamental questions even though we do not know all the answers. This volume does not pretend to be an authoritative pronouncement on behalf of "The Church" but a report from one stage in the pilgrimage of an individual churchman. For twenty years, fifteen of them spent in teaching at church-related colleges and seminaries, I have been engaged in a quest for elusive clues to the churches' responsibilities in relation to the mass media. For more than seven years I have enjoyed the tremendous advantage of associating regularly with the thoughtful, devoted, and enterprising broadcasting staffs of the various denominations and of the National Council of Churches of Christ in the U.S.A. I am particularly indebted to S. Franklin Mack, Richard Sutcliffe, Everett Parker, Harry Spencer, Clayton Griswold, Ben Wilbur, the late Albert Crews, Keith Woolard, Charles Schmitz, Alfred Edyvean, and Lauris Whitman. My students from both at home and abroad have refined my ideas with their challenges and contributions, and my colleagues on the Union Theological Seminary faculty have provided secure health insurance against any Madison Avenue contagion. I am grateful for many provocative conversations with Malcolm Boyd and William Millard.

More recently I have been caught up in the deliberations of the National Council of Churches' Study Commission on the Role of Radio, Television, and Films in Religion, the members of which encouraged and commissioned me to undertake the writing of this manuscript.

I have been so influenced by sharing ideas with this group that many paragraphs in the following pages, beyond the ones formally acknowledged in footnotes, are probably traceable to one or more of my colleagues on the Commission. I am conscious of the direct assistance of R. H. Edwin Espy, Davidson Taylor, David Barry, Rome Betts, Robert Spike, Walter Emery, Joseph Sittler, Dallas Smythe, J. Edward Sproul, Murray Stedman, Leila Anderson, Joseph Klapper, Herbert Evans, and D. Campbell Wycoff, but other members also contributed much to discussions which illuminated various issues.

My wife not only has helped in the preparation of the actual manuscript but has managed household affairs in Massachusetts, New York, and London in such a way as to make its completion possible.

Contents

xv

Contents

CHAPTER **1**

A Christian's View of the Media

No one knows exactly how powerful are radio and television as instruments of influence in twentieth-century America. They are pervasive—more than 80 per cent of all American homes are equipped with television and more than 98 per cent have radios. They are time-consuming—most listener-viewers spend more time with their electronic boxes than with any other waking activity except working, and with the reduction in working hours and retirement age even this exception may eventually disappear. They exert many demonstrable, superficial influences: they create celebrities, popularize songs, and instigate passing crazes such as hoola hooping.

19

But what basic differences do they make in the lives of individuals and in the structure of our society? Even the experts do not really know. Available research into the effects of the media is limited and, at crucial points, inconclusive. Casual observers are likely to underestimate the probable influence in some respects, exaggerate it in others. Even the most thoughtful analysts may be pushed by the newness of the media toward positions of optimism or pessimism, depending on their tendencies to welcome or resist cultural innovations. However, no matter how enthusiasts and critics differ in their evaluation of the nature and extent of the influence, there is mutual acknowledgment that the influence is undoubtedly substantial.

There is general agreement among researchers that the more personal the medium the more effective it is likely to be in channeling communication. Thus, the give-and-take of personal conversation is superior to one-way broadcasting which, in turn, has advantages over the printed media. This, of course, is a generalization which has many exceptions. Books, for example, possess a distinctive scholarly efficiency because they can use the shorthand of symbols to convey abstractions at rates of speed which vary with the abilities of readers; they can be preserved, catalogued, and indexed with comparative ease.

The personal factor, however, is important to any form of communication and on this point broadcasting is strong in comparison with other technical developments. Both radio and television convey the emotional overtones of sound, including the human voice, both offer an immediacy which connects the event directly with the perceiver, and television adds the dimensions of sight and motion.

It is thus not too fantastic when Marshall McLuhan refers to our "post-literate" culture and offers the opinion, "Television may be as decisively the successor to writing as oral speech was the predecessor of writing."[*1]

Such an observation is especially provocative in the light of Harold Innis' theory that, historically, empires rested on technologies of communication. According to Mr. Innis, whenever there is a far-reaching change in means of communication, a social change of consequence must occur, such as the Reformation following the development of printing. He also voices the opinion that we are moving from a print culture to an electronic culture.[2]

How do Christians react to the advent of an electronic culture? What is the responsibility of the church in a world influenced by these new media? In past years there has been little awareness of the problem. More recently, however, there has been a stirring of interest and concern, often in the local congregation. It may begin with the realization that children are singing beer commercials with more enthusiasm than hymns, or that cowboys, private detectives, and comedians are better known in the church school than prophets and apostles, or that it is foolhardy to schedule a group meeting in competition with GUNSMOKE. Laymen, along with pastors and denominational executives, are beginning to press for action on behalf of the church with respect to the mass media.

One familiar result is the appointment of a national denominational committee which recommends the allocation of a broadcasting budget and the establishment of a department. With or without the co-operation of other denominations the new department produces a series of

---

* All numbered references for each chapter are found at the end of the book as Appendix C: Notes by Chapters.

telecasts which, it is hoped, will justify an early increase in the departmental budget.

All these steps within ecclesiastical organizations are desirable and even necessary, but they are not enough unless they enlist pastors, teachers, and group leaders to take an active interest in all that is happening nationally and locally in terms of radio and television. The churches' responsibility in the world of radio and television goes far beyond the production and distribution of a few religious programs. There is need for thoughtful response, in the light of Christian faith, to all the programs and policies of the media.

Current attitudes of many churchmen toward radio and television generally reveal a misunderstanding of either the media or Christian faith or both. Their attitudes may be classified as either daydreams, nightmares, or illusions.

Daydream

The daydreamer is the enthusiast who acclaims radio and television uncritically as a mysterious and fantastically powerful means of evangelism. He overlooks the fact that only an infinitesimal portion of air time is devoted to religion, much of which is of doubtful authenticity, and that the bulk of the program schedule may be creating or at least reinforcing a climate essentially uncongenial for Christianity. The daydreamer who acknowledges this possibility usually advocates that "the children of light" should become wiser in the ways of this world; that the same techniques which sell soap so successfully should be employed to "sell religion." He thus overlooks the fact that there are greater differences than similarities between merchandising products and communicating the Christian faith, and he underestimates the danger of distorting the Gospel in the process of attempting to translate it into terms compatible with the current nature of the mass media in this country. In addition, he overlooks audience factors which make it extremely difficult to employ the mass media to change attitudes.

Nightmare

While unconditional enthusiasm for radio and television is a form of daydreaming, indiscriminate denunciation and renunciation of the media is little more than a nightmare. The broadcasting output is regularly described as vulgar, deceitful, irrresponsible, standardized, manipulative, sensationalistic, escapist, and materialistic, causing many people to use the media as a scapegoat for all the evils of society from juvenile delinquency to political immaturity. It is easier to blame radio and television for the unsocial behavior of children and adults than to search for deeper causes which may be closer to our doorsteps.

This is not to deny that radio and television confront our society with certain dangers; we shall explore these in due time. To admit the existence of the problem, however, is no reason for a disdainful dismissal of the mass media from serious consideration by the churches. The person who wishes that he could awake and find that television (or nuclear fission) had not been discovered is resorting to the same sort of escapism of which he accuses the media. A despairing fear of television's manipulative power betrays a lack of confidence in the integrity of God's human creation and an unwitting acceptance of some advertisers' presupposition that man is not "a little lower than the angels" but only a little higher than a guinea pig.

Men who are normally thoughtful in diagnosing other problems of American culture are blindly opinionated with respect to the mass media. "Of course I never watch television *but*" is a familiar prelude to an incredible expression of nonsense from otherwise well-informed persons. Theologians who are sensitive to shades of gray in all other areas of life see only ethical black and white when looking at their TV screens. It has been clear for a long time that in political matters there are choices to be made between evils and that it is less than Christian to take refuge from the necessity of such choices by refusing to support any cause or any party. This principle, however, has not yet been applied by many theologians to the problems of the mass media.

Illusion

In attempting to avoid both naïve optimism and irresponsible pessimism the Christian may accept a view of the media which is little more than an illusion. This is the idea that the media are neutral, that they can be used for good or evil, depending on the user. On the surface this is plausible but in a deeper sense it is a misrepresentation.

As electronic devices radio and television are uncommitted to any particular purpose but as soon as they are incorporated into a social and economic pattern they lose their neutrality. We cannot look very closely at the media *as they exist* in our society without realizing that they have a definite and obvious bias. Different points of view are represented on the air, but the range of expression is limited by the philosophy of the owners and operators of broadcast facilities.

Calling attention to this bias is not an accusation of insidious purposes; in fact, as we shall see in Chapter 2, radio and television tend to reflect prevailing elements in American life. Many of the questionable features of the media have roots in attitudes and values supported by homes, schools, and churches.

Cautioning against the illusion of neutral media, therefore, is not intended to start a search for villains. There should be a search for standards, values, and purposes, but this search must not be confined to the industry. The world of broadcasting is not something totally apart from the churches. Some churchmen own, operate, and perform in the media as occupational expressions of their purpose in life; as listening-viewing citizens almost all churchmen are at least partly responsible, as we shall see, for program offerings; churches as institutions are directly responsible for some of the worst broadcasts now being aired. All of us are involved in the world of radio-television, whether or not we know it or like it.

Vision

A Christian's view of broadcasting should be more realistic than a daydream, less fantastic than a nightmare, and clearer than an illusion. The remaining alternative is vision. The media are seen to be neither magically beneficial nor inevitably degrading; they are part of an imperfect world, subject to perversion but also subject to reclamation and enlistment in fulfillment of the Creator's purposes. Like the rest of the natural world they offer beauties and mysteries to be explored or exploited. Beyond this, however, radio and television constitute a powerful channel for social forces with which we must grapple. At times their influence runs parallel with the objectives of the Christian church, at other times their objectives appear to be uncongenial or antagonistic. There are occasions when Christians, whether broadcasters, listener-viewers, or religious educators, should encourage and assist in carrying out certain policies of the media; there are other occasions when policies should be criticized and opposed.

Perspective for this vision can come from the Christian's position "in the world but not of the world." No matter how deeply we are involved in the world of radio and television our ultimate orientation comes from elsewhere. Having seen God at work in the world neither removing nor overlooking evil but enduring and transforming it, the Christian has been called to do likewise.

It is not surprising, then, that religious groups are giving belated attention to the place of radio and television in our society. When the National Council of Churches of Christ in the U.S.A. established a special study commission on "The Role of Radio, Television, and Films in Religion" supporting statements included the following:

"In spite of the fact that radio, television and films have added a new dimension to life, they remain an appendage to the life of the church. No real attempt has been made to assess their influence on the Christian community. No long-range planning has been done toward a positive integration of these media into the total effort of the church to fulfill its mission in society. . . .

"We recognize that a relatively new and pervasive influence has come into our culture. . . . These new communications media deeply influence all levels of life. . . . The role of interpreting the meaning of life once was largely carried by the church. . . . Now, even though unintentionally, nevertheless inevitably, the mass media of communication participate in this function. The church must make its resources for this interpretive role available, critically and constructively, to the media of communication so that this function is responsibly fulfilled."[3]

One of the earliest apostolic letters of Pope John XXIII stressed the pastoral importance of modern communications media and strengthened the Vatican department in charge of them. He exhorted the hierarchy to pay increased attention to the impact of modern communication techniques on faith, morals, and ecclesiastical discipline. He emphasized the "great possibilities that the cinema, radio, and television offer for the spreading of higher culture, of art worthy of the name and—above all—of truth." He deplored the "moral dangers and damages not infrequently caused" by the media when they offend "Christian morality and the very dignity of man."[4]

Evaluation of the influence of the media is not, by any means, an exclusively religious concern. The conclusions of thoughtful Christians will often coincide with the views of persons who do not acknowledge Christian roots for their social concern. At crucial points, however, the position of the Christian has a foundation in the convictions of his faith concerning the God-man relationship.

The Christian will join with others in encouraging broadcasts which take into account the many dimensions of the human personality, which awaken an individual and broaden his horizons, which stimulate his growth through recreation, inspiration, and enlightenment. He will favor broadcasts which contribute to interpersonal growth and which promote thoughtful discussion of social issues. He will not be alone in discouraging broadcasts which are dehumanizing, which shrink man's perspective, which dull the sensibilities by endless repetition of the commonplace and tawdry. But Christian motivation for these concerns comes from sources deeper than enlightened self-interest, expediency, or even the dignity of man. The Christian is convinced that man is capable of recognizing and fulfilling a function for which he was created. He senses an obligation to account for the use of his unique combination of talents; he feels responsible to God both for his personal development and for his best contribution to the common welfare. Since God himself respects man's freedom and does not manipulate him, the Christian believes that man should do no less in relation to his fellow men.

Knowing the human limitations of listener-viewers the Christian will not be surprised that the programs which seem to have the greatest value will not always be the most popular or the most profitable financially. A similar Christian realism, recognizing the limitations of broadcasters and regulatory officials, will see the need for continual re-examination of our American system of broadcasting.

The church which believes its responsibility in broadcasting is discharged with the production of a few programs is blind to the fact that all the output of radio and television affects the conditions within which churches function; the most important influence on religious attitudes almost undoubtedly comes from "secular" programs. We are deeply concerned with religious programs, and the final three chapters will deal with them, but there are other considerations which are primary and more pressing.

When a church is alerted to the power of the mass media the first reaction may take such forms as these:

- opposition to the portrayal of violence and immorality on the air
- advocacy of more frequent and more complimentary representation of clergymen
- promotion of references to God and goodness in "secular" programs.

All these are justified under certain conditions, but in other cases they may be unworthy of a mature Christian outlook and they will betray a lack of understanding of the nature of radio and television. At best they do not demonstrate a depth and breadth of view which should characterize the Christian church. To probe more deeply into the place of the church in the world of radio-television we shall begin by giving close attention to the characteristics of the media and their place in our social order.

CHAPTER **2**

The American System of Broadcasting

It is possible to conceive of radio and television as instruments which add very little to the substance of communication. Events such as baseball games, concerts, and church services would occur regardless of broadcasting; microphones and cameras simply make them accessible, without substantial change, to larger publics than could otherwise experience them. Are these media, then, mere transmitters of programs whose real creators come from the theater, music, sports, politics, journalism, education, and religion? Is the function of the mass media simply to convey or perhaps to multiply the influence of the originators of communication?

Not Transmitters but Transformers

Regular listeners and viewers will sense immediately one weakness in this position, the fact that the type of program cited in the paragraph above constitutes only a small fraction of the ordinary station schedule. Most programs are produced especially for radio and television by persons whose major income is derived from the media.

Clergymen, musicians, and politicians who engage in any broadcasting will see a deeper fallacy. It is a rare broadcast that is aired without substantial change. The minister who speaks over the radio on the typical morning devotional series is warned that he must allow the demands of the media to affect his timing and his choice of language; the newspictures of political figures submitting to make-up artists in preparation for television cameras are only symptomatic of basic alterations made in conventions and other political events. Wrestling matches are carefully timed, and even scripted for television. Radio and television are not simply transmitters but transformers. Whenever radio and television "cover" a happening, they color it.

The Ancestry of the Magical Box

The mere fact that a program reaches a person through a radio or television receiver may affect his response to it. The response will differ with the person, but it will be conditioned by his particular attitude toward the media.

Harman Grisewood of the British Broadcasting Corporation maintains that radio and television, products of the Scientific Age, are part of a trend potentially alien to Chris-

tianity. Even though he acknowledges the spurious origins of the old conflict between science and religion Mr. Grisewood sees the electronic inventions as perpetuators of a discredited but persistent mechanistic outlook. The mystical qualities of a box able to pick up sound and pictures out of the air would seem to support the dream that man is the master of his fate if only he can continue to unlock nature's secrets. Mr. Grisewood has said, "Wireless and television are no better off in their ancestry than the H-bomb. They are natural, congenial one ought to say, in a wholly secularized, wholly materialist society. . . . In their effects they—however it may be true that they need not be—are powerful agents toward the further materialization of the minds of men. . . . They are part of a godless technocracy."[1]

As if to support Mr. Grisewood's warning the documentary, *"Hemo the Magnificent,"* in the nationally televised TELEVISION SCIENCE SERIES, climaxed its account of blood, its circulation, and the role of the heart with a choir and narrator paying tribute to "science, faith, and hope." Both a scientist ("Ye must have faith") and Paul ("Prove all things; hold fast to that which is good") were quoted. There is little doubt that the media could provide ideal liturgical forms for a cult of scientism, holding that all human problems are ultimately soluble through applying the experimental and manipulative methods of physical science.

To recognize this possibility is not to admit its inevitability. Mr. Grisewood agrees that the Christian who can see the infinite possibilities beyond his own deep, interior dislocation will not easily concede that one of man's discoveries is beyond reclamation. Greater understanding and control of the physical world is surely a part of the divine

will for man in his history; and the communications revolution represents a substantial and unprecedented growth in man's capacities, for whatever purposes used.

Do the Media Change? Reflect? Reinforce?

For what purposes *are* the media being used? We have already noted that they are acclaimed and condemned with nearly equal vigor. To what extent are the media responsible for accomplishments credited to them and for the degradation of which they are accused?

Do the media, by themselves, initiate and accomplish individual and social changes for good or evil? Or do the media only reflect existing attitudes and conditions? Does the reflection bring about any changes or only reinforce what is being reflected? Both critics and supporters of the media are likely to shift position with respect to these questions depending upon the specific subject under consideration. The media boast of creating audiences for classical music and Shakespeare, but claim they only respond to the demand when they offer Westerns and mysteries.

Available research indicates that mass communication does have powerful effects, but that these effects are limited. Radio and television play a role in attitude change, but the more deep-seated the attitude the less likely the change. The commonest effect of mass communication appears to be reinforcement of existing attitudes. Joseph Klapper says, "Mass communication appears to be far more likely to buttress the existing attitudes of its audience than it does to change their ideas or awaken them to any new ideas."[2]

This limitation of the media in accomplishing great changes is partly due to what Dallas Smythe calls "the

resiliency of the individual, stemming from his native common sense."[3] Lest this be interpreted in too optimistic a fashion Dr. Smythe cautions that the experience of Nazi Germany indicates that this resiliency may be overcome if the pressures are strong enough. This is in line with Lazarsfeld and Merton's observation that the media are especially effective when they are monopolistic.

The media are more likely to reinforce than to change attitudes because people tend to choose programs and to pay attention to features within programs which agree with their existing views and interests. People will also remember far more when they agree, and forget when they do not agree with what is being presented. In political campaigns Republicans tend to listen to Republican speeches, Democrats to Democratic speeches; in programs where both parties are represented, Republicans will select and remember statements supporting the Republican position, and vice versa.

The media are seldom the *sole* cause for the development or change of an attitude; a person is more directly influenced by groups to which he belongs and by local "opinion leaders" whom he respects. Broadcasting lacks direct "give-and-take" and the effects of the media are ordinarily filtered through other agencies such as the family, the church, or the knowledgeable neighbor.

Nevertheless, the media do bring about some measureable changes, and it is important not to be misled by mere percentages in research statistics. When it is reported that a certain broadcast has changed the opinions of only 5 per cent of its audience this may sound insignificant until it is remembered that (1) change in attitude is not a common occurrence in any form of communication, including the pulpit and classroom, and 5 per cent may

be a perfectly respectable figure; (2) a single network television program often attracts twenty million or more viewers, 5 per cent of whom would total a million, a very large number indeed; (3) the effect of the program may be cumulative because the million influenced directly by it may spread the influence among relatives, friends, and co-workers, and (4) the nineteen million unaffected by one program will be exposed to many other broadcasts in the same week, one of which may have more influence on them.

It is possible, too, that the media are making deep, gradual changes which are beyond the observation of contemporary research. Present sociological and psychological measurements may be inadequate for tracing accurately the deepest of attitudes, changes in which may involve years and even decades. The thoughtful observations of parents, pastors, and educators may be more significant than statistical findings of some carefully controlled experiments which rule out crucial factors along with the variables. It must be admitted, however, that there will always be a difficulty in distinguishing "thoughtful observations" from hasty generalizations.

There is some uncertainty, then, concerning the long-range influence of the media. Their power is clear in some respects, doubtful in others. It is entirely possible that the "fall-out" of radio and television—their subtle influence in ways beyond our present calculation—may be of great significance. What is being done to discover all that can be known about the social influence of the media? Meanwhile, how is the power of radio and television being used? What precautions are being taken to assure the operation of stations by responsible citizens?

These questions call for a review of present national

policies concerning the licensing and regulation of stations and for an examination of working principles which govern the operation of broadcasting.

Background of Government Regulation

Radio and television stations use frequencies and channels which belong to the public. Not everyone may build and operate a radio station; if there were no restrictions on the use of the air waves there would be dreadful interference. This, in fact, was the chaotic condition in the early nineteen twenties when it became obvious that the government must exercise some responsibility. In one situation in 1922 two Washington stations broadcast on three successive Sundays services from two churches at the same time on the same wave length.

In 1925 Herbert Hoover as Secretary of Commerce stated a philosophy which became the basis for government regulation of broadcasting. He maintained that "the ether is a public medium, and its use must be for public benefit," that the main "consideration in the radio field is, and always will be, the great body of the listening public, millions in number, country-wide in distribution."[4]

Out of the conferences which Hoover sponsored came the Radio Act of 1927 which established the principle that the radio spectrum belongs to the public and that a broadcaster is merely licensed to use a particular frequency for a specified period of time but acquires no ownership rights to that frequency. His use of the frequency is subject to periodic reconsideration. The Communications Act of 1934, establishing the Federal Communications Commission (FCC), expanded the same principles.

Difficulties in Regulation

Since the government thus has authority to grant and renew licenses there must be standards by which such decisions can be made; this is an area of considerable uncertainty which has been a matter of concern to both government and industry. There are at least three sources of difficulty in the effective regulation of stations by the Federal Communications Commission.

The first is the ambiguity in the statutory provisions relating to the Commission's powers and responsibilities. The law provides that licenses for station operation may be granted and renewed only if the "public interest, convenience, and necessity" will be served. But there are wide differences of opinion as to the meaning of these terms. The phrase must also be interpreted in the light of Section 326 of the Communications Act, which reads:

> Nothing in this Act shall be understood or construed to give the Commission the power of censorship over the radio communications . . . and no regulation or condition shall be promulgated or fixed by the Commission which shall interfere with the right of free speech by means of radio communication.[5]

At least one commissioner, T. A. M. Craven, has taken the stand that this section of the Act, along with the First Amendment, prohibits the Commission from exercising any authority over broadcast programing except in cases where there are violations of specific laws, such as those prohibiting libel and lotteries. However, as Walter Emery has pointed out in his historical discussion of the FCC, the Commission has, from the beginning, taken the attitude that it does have the power to take into account program service as an important factor in its public interest determinations. Mr. Emery contrasts the position taken by Commissioner Craven with the views of other commissioners who "have interpreted Section 326 differently. Relating it to other provisions of the Act, they believe that, while the Commission cannot tell a station what particular program or programs it can or cannot present, it does have the authority and the responsibility to review the over-all operation of a station when it comes up for renewal of its license to determine whether its operation has been in the public interest. This interpretation seems to be correct as confirmed by the legislative history of the Radio Act of 1927, the Communications Act of 1934, and the consistent administrative practice of the two commissions and court decisions."[6]

In 1934 an official spokesman of the National Association of Broadcasters, speaking to a congressional committee on behalf of the industry, supported this position:

> It is the manifest duty of the licensing authority in passing upon applications for licenses or the renewal thereof, to determine whether or not the applicant is rendering or can render an adequate public service. Such service necessarily includes broadcasting of a considerable portion of programs devoted to education, religion, labor, agricultural and similar activities concerned with human betterment.[7]

Contrary to this, Mr. Craven has proposed that the Commission should leave programing exclusively in the hands of the broadcaster and not inquire in any way as to the over-all balance between different types of presentations. The chief basis for Commissioner Craven's view is his belief that the FCC violates traditional concepts and constitutional guarantees of free speech, and exercises undue control when it attempts to regulate programing.

The New York Times broadcasting columnist Jack Gould, however, expressed another concern when he wrote, "Were Mr. Craven's proposal to be adopted, it would practically complete the FCC's abdication of responsibility for broadcasting and turn it entirely over to those being licensed."[8] These differing viewpoints thus pose the age-old critical problem of democratic government: how to achieve effective regulation without violating freedom and individual responsibility. It is obvious that although the Commission does exercise some control over broadcast programing, the ambiguity of present laws has definitely been a limiting factor. The regulatory situation is further complicated by an ambivalent Congress which blows both hot and cold on the question.

Even if its regulatory power in this regard were perfectly clear the Commission would be handicapped by a second difficulty, its heavy work load and small staff. The FCC must deal not only with all forms of broadcasting, including standard radio, frequency modulation, television, and a host of special and auxiliary services such as those associated with amateurs, police patrol, and taxicabs, but with a gigantic telegraph and telephone industry. It is not surprising that there is always a huge backlog of unfinished business and that not all actions reflect the most careful consideration of the Federal Communications Commissioners.

A third difficulty is the problem of maintaining the quasi-judicial character of the regulatory agency in the face of pressures from industry, the White House, and Congress, some members of which have financial interests in broadcasting stations. A Special Subcommittee on Legislative Oversight of the House of Representatives has called attention to this problem.

The Commission, then, is handicapped by some ambiguity concerning its authority, by an excessive work load, and by powerful outside pressures. As a result there has been little active concern on the part of the FCC in recent years with program standards. A top network executive has remarked that if the Communications Act were abolished it would make little or no difference in programing policies of stations. He meant the statement to be a tribute to the broadcasters' own sense of responsibility, but it also demonstrates a disregard for an agency which is supposed to represent the interests of the public, the actual owner of the air waves.

Self-Regulation

Most broadcasters themselves advocate self-regulation and the National Association of Broadcasters (NAB) (formerly titled "of Radio and Television Broadcasters") has codes for both radio and television dealing with program and advertising content. However, subscription to the codes is voluntary, with about two-thirds of the country's stations participating, and the enforcement procedures are not strong. Nor can any formal code be expected to have much effect on a broadcaster who desires to evade it.

Thoughtful broadcasters would be the first to agree that neither the FCC nor the NAB exerts significant influence on program schedules. In the last analysis the primary responsibility for station operation has rested with owners and their employees. In examining the nature of the media, then, our search narrows to the crucial point of management. What are the prevailing policies of management? At this point we are concentrating attention on commercial stations, delaying until later chapters a consideration of educational outlets.

The Position of Management

Most American radio and television stations are operated as business enterprises with one major purpose: to earn money for stockholders and employees. In a very real sense they have their own goals, creed, ethics, and even forms of evangelism. Lazarsfeld and Merton pointed out more than ten years ago that the mass media are integrated into the national business community and shelter that community generally from criticism through (1) the narcotic effect of their product and (2) excluding or softening criticism of the social system.[9] From his experience in industry Leo Bogart agrees that the popular arts "tend to be conservative in their overt political and social contents, since it is dangerous to offend any sizable portion of the audience by questioning its established values or beliefs. Another reason for the conservativism of the mass media is that as commercial institutions they are part of a business community whose predominantly conservative thinking very often contrasts with the traditional role of the artist as critic of the social order."[10] This does not mean that a particular philosophy is legislated upon employees but that it permeates an organization through example and rewards.

The Influence of Advertising

It can be maintained that the real control of broadcasting lies not with owners and operators of stations but with advertisers and advertising agencies. The owners are legally responsible and most of them want their stations to be more than mere conduits, but the pressure of sponsors is understandably great. Unlike newspapers and magazines radio and television maintain little separation between content and advertising. Advertisers refuse to buy programs of which they do not approve, exercise close control over the ones they do sponsor, and insure compliance with their wishes through threat of cancellation.

Max Lerner maintains: "The broadcasters have chosen to take the subsidy largely on the advertiser's terms, giving him control not only over his advertising time and commercials, but over the nature and even the content of the program. This was a fateful choice and an unavoidable one. As a result the broadcasters not only sell advertising time but sell the audience as well—and themselves."[11]

But does it really make any difference whether stations control programing or whether it is controlled through advertisers and their agencies? The separation of advertising from news which theoretically frees the press from outside domination does not motivate sensationalist dailies to portray life as anything more than a series of scandals, crimes, and cheap erotic pleasures. In the desire to reach as many readers, viewers, or listeners as possible the interests of management and advertising are identical. On the positive side, it is possible for an advertiser to be just as responsive to the public interest as a station manager.

The missing factor in this line of argument is the moral and legal responsibility of the broadcaster to operate more than an advertising business. He is providing a public service, in connection with which it is anticipated that he will be able to make a reasonable profit. Llewelyn White, on behalf of the Commission on Freedom of the Press, comments on the tension between these two functions, a tension painfully familiar to every sensitive program executive in the media:

> It must be fairly obvious that not everything that the average American requires to enable him to understand and perform his increased duties as a citizen will, in terms of radio programs, sell goods and services. . . . Let us be frank about it: What we have here is a continuing contest between two diametrically opposed approaches to the problem of public service in radio—one based on long-range citizen needs as a criterion, the other based on Hooper ratings and sales charts.[12]

On the one hand, then, the business of a station is to sell products. To do this it must deliver to the sponsor audiences, the larger the better. In view of modern capital investment and time costs ($125,000 per hour on a TV network) the audiences must be vast indeed.

Emphasis on Audience Size

This is readily admitted by broadcasters. It is, in fact, the fundamental program principle. Richard Salant, Columbia Broadcasting System vice-president, has said, "The fact is that broadcasting is a truly mass medium. It has to be. Unless it can enlist and hold the interest of most of the people, a good part of the time, it is just too expensive a medium to survive. It must, in its spectrum of programing, have something—even the great majority of its material—that will appeal to not just thousands or hundreds of thousands but to millions and tens of millions."[13]

On the other hand, the station is operating on a frequency belonging to the public. Is there here any real conflict of interest? Or is the public interest best served by programs which satisfy the tastes of the largest possible numbers?

43

There is nothing inherently wrong with programs which attract large audiences. Some of the most worthwhile broadcasts on the air attract substantial numbers of listener-viewers. But there are different ways of attracting people, and the easiest ways may be debasing. To attract people to better programs may require years of exposure —a difficult requirement for a medium oriented to immediate sales results.

It is obvious that radio and television must be concerned with numbers of viewers and listeners. But must this lead to a situation where the media offer to all of the people much of the time what most of the people want only some of the time? Some of the most familiar, most persistent criticism of broadcasting is directed to the search for the lowest common denominator, which may ignore any purposes or meaning deeper than sales. A Chicago disc jockey said: "I'm sincere. I have integrity. Nine out of ten records I play, I don't think are good records. I play the things they want to hear. Unless I do, I don't have an audience, and therefore I have denied my station, my second integrity, an audience. And the station loses the account of my advertiser, my third integrity. But they're all wrapped up into one integrity—to build the biggest audience there is."[14] The twisted use of the word "integrity" is symptomatic of a value system which has its own standards, far removed from the Christian ethic.

The Christian church is not intent upon developing longhairs and snobs, but there is a legitimate concern for broadcasts which fulfill the potentialities of the media, of the persons who create the programs, and of the listener-viewers. This is an elementary matter of stewardship. David Barry has suggested that the media are being used for rather petty purposes in comparison with their potentialities. He makes it clear that "the critical word is 'petty,' not 'evil.' It is as though the chief use of nuclear power were to operate a series of amusement parks."[15]

It is possible to agree with Dr. Barry without losing sight of the difficulty facing the broadcasting industry. The Christian is fully aware of the ease with which man can be attracted by the petty, the transient, the inconsequential. The programs of many churches are crammed with petty activities. The occupant of the organizational manse is not in the best possible position to pass judgment on anyone else for preoccupation with the superficial in pursuit of numbers.

Beyond the Pursuit of Numbers

In theory the industry has acknowledged the need for programs which attract fewer than the largest possible number of listener-viewers. Robert W. Sarnoff, chairman of the board of the National Broadcasting Company, has stated as the first fundamental belief of the industry that "broadcasting, as a mass medium, best serves the public interest through programing which meets the desires and interests of the majority of people," but his second fundamental is that "broadcasting assumes a secondary function of programing for minority tastes and interests, and by doing so, offers the majority continuing opportunity to absorb new interests."[16] The networks claim that their schedules include more programs for minority tastes than would be apportioned on a strict basis of numerical representation. Thus if 2 per cent of radio listeners appreciate operatic broadcasts perhaps 3 or 4 per cent of the schedule is devoted to them. It is obvious that this principle applies in some areas of programing and not in others. It must be remembered that most of these programs for minority tastes are unsponsored and the local outlets of the network are quite likely to substitute for them commercial programs similar in appeal to the majority of the network offerings.

It should also be noted that few programs for minority tastes are offered at the most convenient times for listener-viewers. It was even impossible for the Firestone Tire and Rubber Company to continue to buy prime time on any of the networks for a musical program which admittedly attracted smaller audiences than some other broadcasts. For thirty-one years the sponsor served a chosen segment of the total audience, but in 1959 was unable to buy time on any night between 7:30 and 10:30 P.M. because the networks were afraid that even one program with a comparatively limited audience might affect the ratings of other programs on the same network that evening. The VOICE OF FIRESTONE case illustrates one of the foremost problems confronting TV: how to find even just a little time within the prime evening viewing hours for minority programing.

Some persons in the industry see the continual emphasis on "majority" programing as poor business. They point out that there is virtually no such thing as a majority audience, that there are only various sizes of minority audiences, and that the ordinary run of programs often attracts the *same*, large minority, to the exclusion of smaller but significant groups. Sylvester L. (Pat) Weaver, Jr., former president and chairman of the board of NBC, has condemned the inability of the networks to "understand advertising and the media, which makes them fall into the trap of being solely concerned with the size of the heavy-viewer audience and to make decisions which will eventually degrade their service and break their (advertising) rates." He asks rhetorically, "Are we using too much of our limited time for one kind of entertainment? Are we 'mesmoronizing' large audiences, to an ever-declining percentage of all people in all homes?"[17]

John P. Cunningham, advertising agency president, holds a similar view. He refers to an occasion when a Shakespearean telecast was outrated by Lucille Ball, 41.6 to 10.9. He maintains that this "failure," by ordinary industry measurements, is no reason, even from an advertising standpoint, to avoid Shakespeare on television. Referring to the fact that the rating of 10.9 probably represented about fifteen million people he says, "The 10,000,-000 to 20,000,000 people who like Shakespeare better than Lucy have every right to their minor share of their own airwaves. This kind of program isolates the right markets in the right mood for certain products. Some of us may want access to those markets. Even those who don't, want a full-rounded medium, not a narrow-based one."[18]

Some broadcasters have another reason for believing that program standards should go beyond audience size. The Westinghouse Broadcasting Company, owner of various radio and TV stations, has held conferences on public-service programing attended by hundreds of delegates from commercial stations. At one such meeting the Westinghouse president, Donald H. McGannon, said, "We do believe that public service is good business and have long maintained in our advertising that 'broadcasting is most effective on stations that have earned the respect and confidence of the communities they serve.' "[19]

But is "public relations" or "good business" sufficient motivation for operating a powerful communications system in the best interests of a society? Contrary to false prophets of all centuries including the twentieth, integrity and faithfulness do not guarantee prosperity and popularity. The station manager for whose religion the cross is the central symbol should not be surprised if his advertising revenue is less than that of a competitor whose program standards seem to reflect less concern for the public interest.

This is not to imply that the church member is always the most public-minded program executive. But even when a person does take his Christian commitment seriously he cannot forget that his employees and his stockholders may not share his convictions, nor do many of his listener-viewers. His decisions will not be easy ones. He will, however, be interested in factors other than audience size and sales charts. He will be alert to discover the deeper influences of his station's programs on the people in his community.

One of the discouraging aspects of present conditions in American broadcasting is that the industry is conducting almost no research into the long-range, fundamental influences of the media. In the twentieth century our missiles are guided, but our radio-television transmissions have no comparable sense of direction. Large sums are being spent to measure audiences and to discover how best to sell products to them, but there is almost no careful study of the over-all impact of the media on our society. Network executives have speculated publicly about the desirability of such an investigation, but so far it has had a very low priority. Of course the presuppositions and design of such a study would be of tremendous importance. A superficial job would be worse than none because it would be dangerously misleading.

Industry's apparent unconcern for such basic information lends support to Dallas Smythe's contention, "Power to command something approaching a monopoly of people's sensory attention is vested in a system of organized irresponsibility for its consequences. This is not to impute bad motives to anyone. The business organization functions well for its purposes (to make and sell goods). It was not designed to run people's lives."[20]

From the industry comes an answer by the previously quoted John P. Cunningham, cautioning fellow members of the Association of National Advertisers: "As far as we advertisers are concerned, it is a Time for Pause. We are trustees. We must never forget that the airwaves do not belong to the advertisers—nor to the networks—nor to the FCC—nor to the Federal Government. They belong to the people of the United States."[21]

What is the result of this trusteeship in terms of programs? We have observed an uneasy and uneven balance of power among stations, advertisers, the FCC, and the listening-viewing public. The industry's customary criteria of audience size and sales results are scarcely the only standards to be applied to programs. What, then, are other standards, more crucial for the society served by the media? This will be the object of our search in Chapter 3.

49

CHAPTER **3**

Program Possibilities and Problems

There are many different ways of classifying and evaluating radio and television programs. Each system has its strengths and weaknesses.

Eric Sevareid, speaking at the "Emmy" Award presentations in 1958, evaluated the achievements of television in terms of four functions. In its function *to amuse* he said the industry is doing "very well." In attempting *to inform* he said television was doing "fairly well, and improving." In the endeavor *to educate* he indicated "much is still needed" and he said the industry had "hardly begun" the effort *to inspire*.

Such a division according to function serves some purpose, especially because the emphasis on sales is so likely to mesh with the function to amuse that this single purpose may receive undue attention unless the others are kept in mind as essential to the operation of a broadcasting system "in the public interest, convenience, and necessity."

However, any such functional division has one notable weakness. Its separations do not take into account the fact that the programs intended to amuse may actually inform, educate, or inspire. There is good reason to believe that programs produced only to entertain and sell products may be the most influential in subtle ways. Persons are usually most susceptible to influence from sources which are not identified as deliberately educational or inspirational. The exclusive preoccupation with "entertainment" is so all-pervasive that it infects even the public-service programing—on the assumption that only thus is an audience to be secured. Mr. Severeid's division is important in suggesting that there should be some sort of balance among accepted functions of the media, but any evaluation of programs must dig underneath such external classifications.

Attempts at Evaluation and Classification

The same qualifications must be applied to a similar but simpler division of broadcasts into "serious" and "light" or "entertainment" programs. There is, again, some purpose for making this distinction. Some broadcasters maintain that the mass media are effective only in transmitting the lightest of material, requiring little thought on the part of listener-viewers. Although contradicted by overwhelming evidence this position is so firmly entrenched that it must receive continual bombardment if it is ever to be evacuated. The concept of "entertainment" is often so limited to trivial, superficial, escapist programs that there is justification for suggesting that this is not the entire scope of broadcasting.

Here, again, however, a false division may be implied. Light programs may have very serious purposes, or at least results. What appears to one listener to be a serious program may actually be light entertainment for another. There is also the danger that a program may be classified as serious when it is merely dull and pedantic.

Still another attempt at classification combines format, content, and program type: mystery, Western, classical music, popular music, quiz, variety, news, religion, serious drama, situation comedy, and so on. As soon as one or two programs of a particular type achieve high ratings the air is flooded with imitations. Thoughtful executives in broadcasting are quick to point out that this is evidence of a low level of creativity and creates a saturation which can lead only to boredom. There is a place for Westerns on television, but thirty-two in one season would seem to be more than enough.

It is not sufficient, however, to classify and count the various programs in each category and then recommend adjustments to be made in terms of program balance. Even if the industry would follow such a procedure, which will not happen, major questions are left unanswered. Greater distinctions are to be made among programs of a single type than between types as such. There is nothing inherently evil in Westerns and mysteries, nor are talks and discussions inevitably valuable.

Joseph Sittler has compared two Westerns, THE LONE RANGER and GUNSMOKE:

The Lone Ranger is a Messianic figure. He always appears as by advent in the midst of trouble. He is the deliverer from predicaments. And, like God the Father (Deus Absconditus), the Deliverer is always masked. He is confident, unambiguous in his reading of and his acting in the given moral situation. He never uses violence to gain his end; if he shoots it is not to kill but to disarm; he appears on a great white horse, handles human error, stupidity, evil as from an olympian righteousness, performs the needed deeds of liberation, and, as the play ends, disappears in a kind of mystical ascent with the promise of a parousia when men again get themselves into a hopeless mess.

Superior to THE LONE RANGER in sheer actuality is the program, GUNSMOKE. Marshall Dillon is no God-figure. He is a capable, modest, wise, unpontifical servant of the State. The situations into which he is drawn are concrete, broadly human, complex. He is not able to liberate from all imprisonments, save all lives, solve all problems, wipe away all tears, preserve all values, or set all things right. In the name of proximate justice, a better order of tolerable goods, he starts with the given and works toward a possible solution—and only occasionally finds it.[1]

Charles J. Rolo has attempted a similarly provocative analysis of mysteries. It is his hypothesis "that the murder mystery is, in essence, a metaphysical success story." He adds:

Every murder mystery poses symbolically the problem of Evil—and resolves it; every detective story therefore meets a deep metaphysical need. . . . The detective story is modern man's Passion Play. . . . Mystery stories are blood-stained fairy tales which enact the cycle, Paradise Lost—Paradise Sought For—Paradise Regained. They allow us to play, vicariously, the role of different kinds of Saviour.[2]

Such analyses raise more questions than they answer, but they do demonstrate the inadequacy of another division common among churchmen, one which would classify programs as "objectionable" or "unobjectionable." According to this system any broadcasting is objectionable if it includes profanity, drunkenness (unless the victim becomes a member of Alcoholics Anonymous), murder (if left unpunished), uncomplimentary treatment of religion and clergymen, or almost any reference to sex. (The Bible, of course, would not stand up very well under such a code.) Broadcasting, as a home medium, has been unusually aware of these canons, but the result is often that programs are regarded as unobjectionable or wholesome when they are merely inane. Some of the most thoughtful writers of our generation are discouraged from applying their creativity to radio and TV because of the restrictiveness of the media.

The worst aspect of this classification system is the narrowness of its scope. It disregards the most significant elements of most programs. William F. Lynch has made a comment which is especially significant coming from a clergyman of the church which supports the Legion of Decency. What he says about films applies equally to radio and television:

At present many producers pay attention to censors or moral theologians, but only as to a limited, external force. What it amounts to is that they will clean up a particular sequence of two minutes out of a vast set of visual images. They are free to let the other ninety-eight minutes of morally indifferent trash remain because the influence of a creative religious intelligence has not yet made itself

54

felt in this area of our society. This influence can become very great, but only if it develops a sympathetic alliance with the artist and understands him from the inside.[3]

The Christian looking for standards by which to evaluate the output of the mass media cannot stop with the commonly accepted ones listed above. Dr. Lynch goes on to suggest others, and Malcolm Boyd also formulates certain criteria worth consideration.[4] The observations of literary and art critics, social scientists and journalists, such as included in the collection, *Mass Culture*, edited by Rosenberg and White, are provocative.[5] Essentially, however, this is a task which will require a great deal of intellectual wrestling among members of the Christian community. A neat formula is neither expected nor desired, but few Christians yet see as much as a line of direction.

We cannot expect all programs in a pluralistic democracy to be Christian. Some would contend that we cannot expect any program, unless it is our own production, to be distinctively or even explicitly Christian. We can, however, judge programs by criteria which are basic to all religious faiths and to the artistic sensibility which shares an ultimate concern for man's future and destiny in life.

Man or Less-Than-Man

One such criterion is fundamental to all others. It accepts broadcasting's focus on the audience and asks of each program element, is the listener-viewer treated as man or less-than-man? Is he regarded as a man, or as a mouse to be routed through mazes? Is he a man, or a machine to be operated, a vegetable to be cultivated? Is he a man capable of growing and learning, or simply a creature able to react? If he is regarded as a man he should be aroused and stimulated rather than stupefied; his horizons should be enlarged rather than shrunk; he should be exalted rather than degraded.

This criterion goes beyond the concept of exploitation or manipulation, which suggests a deliberate attempt by the broadcaster to make a puppet out of a person. Important though this is, it neglects (1) the influences which are anything but deliberate but which, nevertheless, tend to make a listener-viewer less-than-man and (2) the positive aspects of a broadcaster's responsibility and opportunity to treat a listener-viewer as true man.

Here, then, is a standard which takes into account the best interests of society. It is a standard which the church itself could often apply more rigorously in its own behavior patterns. It should be acceptable to thoughtful non-Christians although the Christian can claim that it is derived from the Hebrew-Christian view of man in his relationship to God. Let us see how it applies to various radio-TV program elements which we shall divide, for the sake of convenience, into advertising, news, and entertainment.

Advertising: Information or Misinformation

Can the commercial content of broadcasting help a man to grow in any significant way, or does it tend to make him less-than-man? On an elementary level the advertiser would claim that listener-viewers can learn much from commercials. Informational advertising can make possible a comparison among products which allows the consumer to make discriminating selections and stimulates a manufacturer to make continuing improvements. At the very least it establishes brand names as symbols of quality and reliability.

But how much of radio-TV advertising deals with significant differences among products? Broadcast advertising is severely limited by time and space and the bulk of it is devoted to soap, cigarettes, automobiles, and similar highly competitive fields where all leading brands may be comparable in quality and cost. The advertiser frequently invents something new to claim for one as opposed to another, hence the ludicrous laboratory tests and testimonies. In the absence of real differences among products there is resort to sly deceit ("Three out of four doctors prescribe the *ingredients* in Anacin"), and repetitious gobbledygook ("Lanolin Plus is made by Lanolin chemists whose specialty is—Lanolin!"). The advertiser is often willing to irritate the listener-viewer in the hope that the brand name will be remembered when the irritation is forgotten.

Advertising: Motivation Research

Knowing that he cannot sell his product on the basis of conscious, intelligent choice the advertiser may employ "motivational research" in an attempt to reduce the level of conscious awareness to the point where a person may be influenced to act without thinking. Thus we have the muscled, tattooed "Marlboro man" and the fantastically incongruous image of the "Thinking man" who "thinks" like everybody else when it comes to filter cigarettes.

Motivational research is not a new concept, of course. It was familiar to the Greek rhetoricians and to Jeremiah who warned against people who "set a trap to catch men." Its contemporary extreme, subliminal perception, is so obviously dehumanizing (although its actual power is evidently narrowly limited) that both congressmen and the National Association of Broadcasters have expressed caution against its indiscriminate introduction to broadcasting.

Subliminal advertising consists of commercial messages flashed so briefly that the viewer is not conscious of seeing or hearing them. The National Association of Broadcasters issued a memorandum on the subject stating, "A very serious question is the reaction of the public to having subliminal advertising thrust upon them. There may well be grave concern over the idea of advertising which affects people below their level of conscious awareness, so that they are not able to exercise conscious control over their acceptance or rejection of the messages.[6] It is interesting to note (1) that the memorandum describes an approach characteristic of much advertising which is not technically subliminal and (2) that the response of the National Association of Broadcasters to this is on the level of public relations ("the reaction of the public") rather than on the level of ethics and social responsibility.

Even in its ordinary forms motivational research causes a writer in the business-oriented *Fortune* magazine to raise "some ethical questions, among them the question whether any manufacturer should exploit, as buying motives, the deepest human frailties that can be dug out by psychoanalytic method." Perrin Stryker asks, "Will the use of such a technique reinforce consumer attitudes and motives that advertisers might better leave alone?" He lists as signs of immaturity revealed by motivational research fears about nonconformity, anxiety over security, narcissism, reluctance to face some of the necessary but disagreeable chores of life and excessive emulation of the Joneses; then he suggests that the real trouble is not that these weaknesses are exposed but that "motivational research often seeks to recommend, openly or implicitly, that U.S. business nourish these weaknesses and pander to them."[7]

It is obvious that the *intention* of *some* advertising is to make of the listener-viewer less-than-man. A continuous barrage of such commercials could conceivably create an unhealthy climate of exaggeration and deceit within which there would be such loss of mutual confidence and trust that the entire social structure would be seriously affected.

Advertising: Resistance

Listener-viewers, however, may not be so susceptible to manipulation as professional motivational researchers claim. One prominent advertising executive has expressed another side of the matter, "Modern sensation writers make ad men sound like a combination of Svengali and Freud. This is just so much hogwash. Anyone who thinks that people can be fooled or pushed around has an inaccurate and pretty low estimate of people and he won't do very well in advertising . . . the question is: is motivational research a boon or a boondoggle?"[8]

From the Christian perspective it must be admitted that man can be and often has been pushed around, but this need not happen. The church has the responsibility not only to oppose attempts at manipulation but also to assist listener-viewers in learning to resist such attempts.

One form of resistance is outright rebellion against sponsors whose advertising is an obvious attempt to deceive. Another form is laughter at the ludicrous ads; this can be especially effective if discrimination is learned in childhood. Perhaps the most common resistance is apathy.

Studies have shown that few listener-viewers have serious objections to commercials as such. There is even a certain amount of prestige associated with a sponsored program in comparison with a sustaining one. But commercials are not regarded as a source of reliable and helpful information; instead they are looked upon as a "necessary evil" to be endured in preference to other ways of financing broadcasting. They are also welcomed by some members of the audience as intermissions making possible the performance of household and personal duties. The classic evidence for this claim comes from water-consumption figures, which were shown in one community to peak phenomenally during the commercial time between programs.

There are frequent objections to the obtrusive placement of commercials which, in itself, can be one form of manipulation, but in the face of audience apathy it is understandable that a sponsor will make every attempt to have his message seen and heard. There are also objections to the number and length of commercials, but brevity is one limiting factor in the informational function of ads. Perhaps critics should consider the possibility of longer announcements provided they be more constructively functional instead of merely repetitive and deceitful.

Sponsors and advertising agencies have good reason to give careful thought to current attitudes toward broadcast advertising. Their business would seem to have a shaky foundation in the audience-attitude that commercials are a necessary evil. Beyond this, the Christian advertiser will have at least as much interest as the listener-viewer in the question as to whether commercials are regarding the audience as men or less-than-men.

Advertising: Distribution of Affluence

In dealing with the informational aspect of advertising we have not yet mentioned what advertising specialists would probably regard as a more basic function, keeping our national economy healthy by expediting the distribution of its prodigious output. Scientific discoveries applied to agriculture, manufacturing, and distribution appear to have made poverty of material things unnecessary in America. The mass media can contribute to the elimination of poverty and of hardship by facilitating the most economical distribution of the best quality of goods and services.

Beyond this, however, many businessmen and economists maintain that the artificial creation and stimulation of wants are necessary for an expanding economy. They go a step further and advocate "expedited obsolescence," the replacement of cars, clothing, and appliances long before they are worn out in order to keep production and distribution facilities occupied. According to this view a fundamental purpose of advertising is the systematic creation of discontent. It is also argued that the staggering billions of dollars spent for broadcast advertising in America actually cost the consumer-audiences little or nothing in view of the low unit costs made possible by mass production made possible, in turn, by advertising.

Does this function of broadcasting develop the potentialities of man or reduce him to less-than-man? Contrary to one popular misconception, the Christian faith is deeply concerned with the material side of life. There is nothing inherently or unconditionally evil about "things." However, an exaggerated and perverted emphasis on the acquisition and possession of things can lead to a corrupted attitude commonly identified as materialism.

August Heckscher maintains, "Goods have become not things to be enjoyed for themselves but symbols of status and symbols of respect. They increase our nervousness instead of increasing our enjoyment of them. What can one say for this modern method of owning goods which is not really owning them at all, discarding them not because they are old or for any other reason but simply because of advertising, group pressure? We become victims of a joyless acquisitiveness."[9]

John Galbraith in *The Affluent Society* takes issue on *economic* grounds with the theory that the artificial creation of wants is desirable and necessary. He claims that an individual's wants cannot be urgent if they must be contrived for him, and that the artificial creation of such wants is therefore a precarious base for economic stability because the purchasing so stimulated is always the first to be cut back in difficult financial times. He attributes all of our economic dangers, including depressions and monetary instability, to a false emphasis on the production of goods at the expense of what he calls "social balance," by which he favors devoting a larger proportion of our national resources to services, education, recreation, and health.[10] Since his theory is contrary to the traditional position of the business community the churches cannot expect much help from broadcasting in considering its possible validity.

We have noted that the advertising functions of the mass media are potentially beneficial to man; broadcasting can contribute to the elimination of poverty and can assist consumers in acquiring good merchandise which is either essential to his life or helpful in the fullest development of his personality. It can also tempt man, however, to a "joyless acquisitiveness" and an unbalanced economy. From Job to Jesus the biblical tradition does not suggest that temptation will ever be legislated out of existence. The Christian does not expect to be relieved of difficult choices in such matters. Neither, however, does the Christian advertiser wish to be identified with the Tempter.

News

Radio and television are also confronted with the issue of treating listener-viewers as men or less-than-men in coverage of news and special events, including politics. It is now possible for persons in remote areas of the country to learn about the most distant places and personalities. It is also possible for them to be given a distorted impression.

The media devote a substantial proportion of broadcast time to news and information. Radio, especially, has a multitude of local and national newscasts, with some stations now devoting a solid block of evening time to extensive news coverage. Radio and TV interview programs, such as MEET THE PRESS and FACE THE NATION, along with televised press conferences, have made it possible for citizens to watch and hear public figures struggle to articulate their positions with respect to many issues. The Murrow-Friendly documentaries have been exceptionally illuminating. Eric Sevareid for CBS and the Huntley-Brinkley team for NBC offer informed interpretation. Few newspapers can equal the survey of foreign affairs conducted by network correspondents at the end of each year.

There is evidence of serious interest on the part of listener-viewers. When President Eisenhower delivered an address on events in Little Rock, Arkansas, an estimated seventy million Americans watched and heard him on the three national television networks. In the fifteen minutes following the address the news commentators of one network did a special analysis of the integration crisis and more than twenty million people tuned to this program, more than watched the competing entertainment attractions on either of the other networks.

In 1958, before he had announced his candidacy for state governor, Nelson Rockefeller was interviewed by Dave Garroway on TODAY. There was a discussion of the study by the Rockefeller Brothers Fund, Inc., which suggested that without immediate action the U. S. might become a second-class power within two years. Mr. Garroway displayed the report in front of the camera and suggested that a copy could be obtained upon request. Within less than a week the network had received two hundred thousand requests for this document dealing with a matter of utmost seriousness.

In attempting to cover the news, radio and television inherit some problems which have long plagued the press and acquire some additional problems which are derived from or at least accentuated by the nature of broadcasting.

Wilbur Schramm, in *Responsibility in Mass Communication,* presents a comprehensive view of the dilemmas facing newsmen in all media when the right of the public to have access to certain information seems to be in conflict with the rights of individuals or groups. When does the public's right to know "the whole story" (1) violate the right of personal privacy? (2) infringe upon an accused person's right? (3) unfairly implicate an innocent person in another's wrongdoing? (4) jeopardize public safety or security?[11] Some newsmen accept responsibility to exercise discrimination in view of such dilemmas. Others argue that the public's right to know must always take precedence, except in times of national military crisis. Otherwise, it is said, the withholding of news is bound to become unfair and capricious, or even to invite unwarranted suspicion.

News: Objectivity

An even more common but equally perplexing problem is the matter of objectivity. It was once thought to be both possible and desirable for a reporter to be "completely objective," to present facts without comment or explanation. Every reporter, however, is somewhat subjective through his selection of material and his use of words. Demagogues also undermine the concept by turning out sensational press releases faster than they can be verified or contradicted. Radio and television are especially susceptible to this exploitation because of their hourly hunger for the latest bulletin. What, then, can the newsman do? Elmer Davis once said:

> The good newsbroadcaster must walk a tightrope between two great gulfs—on one side the false objectivity that takes everything at face value and lets the public be imposed upon by the charlatan with the most brazen front; on the other, the "interpretive" reporting which fails to draw the line between objective and subjective, between a reasonably well-established fact and what the reporter or editor wishes were fact. To say that is easy; to do it is hard.[12]

News: Brevity

The large number of newscasts, especially on radio, gives the impression of extensive news coverage, but the brevity of most programs encourages oversimplification and fragmentation of significant items along with exaggerated emphasis on the sensational, the catastrophic, the accidental, and the peculiar. The latest news receives attention beyond its importance and earlier reports are discarded without careful consideration. Most local stations depend almost entirely on wire services. Where community coverage is attempted it is more likely to deal with routine bulletins than significant issues. The comparatively few stations which employ competent journalists often allocate to them such brief time-periods that they are severely handicapped.

The multiplication of five-minute newscasts on radio goes to the extreme in digesting the digests until what is left is often more deceptive than illuminating. Gunnar Back, director of News and Special Events of WFIL-TV, Philadelphia, has referred to "the censorship of time" in news broadcasts and has said that the daily flow of news over the radio-TV stations "mentions the ideas of our times, without really going into them. . . . We've got the 'who, what, when and where,' but these days there ought to be more of the 'why' in the news."[13]

News: Controversy

To deal with the "why" in the news and thus serve basic needs of man in a modern democratic society a broadcaster finds himself involved in controversy. As a businessman he may wish to avoid this involvement for fear of offending listener-viewers and alienating sponsors. As we shall note later, the businessman is not alone in this respect; many politicians, educators, and clergymen are similarly fearful. If, however, the broadcaster succumbs to the fear, he may use the mass media to reduce listener-viewers to less-than-men, to make them units of insulated ignorance rather than responsible citizens.

Edward R. Murrow made a forthright statement of this problem in speaking to the Radio and Television News Directors' Association. He said:

> I am seized with an abiding fear regarding what these two instruments (radio and television) are doing to our society, our culture and our heritage. . . . If there are any historians about fifty or a hundred years from now, and there are preserved the kinescopes for one week of all three networks, they will find there recorded in black-and-white, or color, evidence of decadence, escapism and insulation from the realities of the world in which we live. . . . Surely we shall pay for using the most powerful instrument of communication to insulate the citizenry from the hard and demanding realities which must be faced if we are to survive. . . . [14]

In opposition to the attitude that "we must at all costs shield the sensitive citizens from anything that is unpleasant" Mr. Murrow is "entirely persuaded that the American public is more reasonable, restrained, and more mature than most of our industry's program planners believe. Their fear of controversy is not warranted by the evidence." He continues:

> I would like to see television to produce some itching pills rather than this endless outpouring of tranquilizers. . . . To a very considerable extent the media of mass communications in a given country reflect the political, economic and social climate in which they flourish. . . . We are currently fat, comfortable and complacent. We have currently a built-in allergy to unpleasant or disturbing information. Our mass media reflect this. But unless we get up off our fat surpluses and recognize that

television in the main is being used to distract, delude, amuse and insulate us, then television and those who work at it, may see a totally different picture too late.[14a]

The comments above must be considered in the light of Mr. Murrow's conviction that "potentially the commercial system of broadcasting as practiced in this country is the best and freest yet devised." Mr. Murrow himself has been responsible for some of the most notable programs ever to deal with controversial issues, including integration and McCarthyism. One presentation in the SEE IT NOW series waded into the controversy over second-class mailing privileges for magazines and newspapers. In the process *Life* magazine, sponsor of Mr. Murrow's PERSON TO PERSON series, was criticized severely by a postal employee who had to deliver the bulky publication. However, the fact that SEE IT NOW was discontinued by the network leads back to the question as to whether such a series is ever likely to be commercially acceptable and, if not, how other provisions can be made for inclusions of such series in program schedules.

It is generally acknowledged that the media played a significant role in resolving the democratic crisis growing from the actions of Senator Joseph McCarthy. Mr. Murrow's documentaries are regarded by some as the turning point in the struggle, but the principal factor was undoubtedly the daily television coverage of the Army-McCarthy congressional hearings, contrasting the bullying tactics of the Senator with the patient reasonableness of the Boston attorney, Joseph Welch. It can be claimed that the broadcasts were essentially melodramas or medieval morality plays, but they at least exposed the public to many aspects of a controversial issue. In recalling them it is sobering to realize that they were carried principally by a network (DuMont) whose schedule was not "handicapped" by the existence of many daytime commercial programs, a condition which contributed to the network's demise. They were also covered as far as Denver by the American Broadcasting Company, then in a much weaker competitive position than at present. NBC televised the hearings only at the beginning, and CBS not at all.

In the Middle East crisis of 1958 both NBC and CBS juggled their schedules to report the swiftly moving events, canceling many commercial programs in the process. Extended live coverage was given deliberations in the United Nations. The dilemma of program executives in making such decisions is highlighted by the commonly reported response to this attempt at public service: many listeners complained because their favorite soap operas had been canceled, but there were few expressions of appreciation.

When a broadcaster deals with more immediate and domestic controversy he is less likely to be received with apathy, but he is more likely to encounter opposition. When Cyrus S. Eaton, interviewed on the air by Mike Wallace, expressed a low opinion of the FBI and of "scores of agencies engaged in investigating, in snooping, in informing, in creeping up on people," Congressman Walter, chairman of the House Committee on Un-American Activities solicited time from the American Broadcasting Company to reply to Mr. Eaton and signed a subpoena for Mr. Eaton to appear before the House Committee.

It should be noted in passing that the "equal time" concept, intended to guarantee fairness in treatment of controversy, may be used instead to avoid controversy. When it is known in advance that one side of an issue is to be presented it can be held, in all solemnity, that a representative of the other side must be invited to appear on the same program. The side that would rather not see an issue discussed in public may then exercise a veto by declining to appear. Thus Dr. David N. Spain, a member of the Study Group on Smoking and Health, was expecting to discuss on Tex McCrary's show on WRCA-TV findings indicating a relationship between cigarettes and cancer until he was told that the producer had been unable to engage a speaker opposing the doctor's views, and Dr. Spain was "disinvited" from the program.

For a brief period the "equal time" concept was also stretched to apply to newscasts. An obscure political candidate complained when his opponent, the mayor of Chicago, appeared in an official capacity on a televised newscast and the FCC ruled that equal time had to be granted the objector. Congress prevented the reoccurrence of such situations by passing legislation exempting newscasts from the "equal time" requirements.

Occasional incidents indicate that broadcasting is less confident of its freedom to treat controversial issues than the press. When CBS in 1957 televised an hour's interview with Nikita S. Khrushchev of the Soviet Union there was so much criticism that the Fund for the Republic authorized a study of the situation by Herbert Mitgang who reported:

If a newspaper had published an interview with Khrushchev, no responsible person in any communications field would have thought of questioning the propriety of the publication, but when a television network, after great precautions to protect the integrity of the performance and after having made its intentions known to the highest level of government, telecast an interview with the

Kremlin leader, the propriety was very seriously questioned. The President of the United States made a statement which at least implied criticism. Important members of Congress openly challenged the wisdom of the presentation. The press was ambivalent.[15]

Mr. Mitgang observed that the networks could be expected to bear such criticism in mind when considering future controversial programs and concluded with an appeal to Congress and Federal agencies to provide more of an atmosphere of freedom.

Commenting to the Connecticut Broadcasters' Association on the Fund for the Republic report, Sig Mickelson, then a CBS vice-president, agreed with Mr. Mitgang's conclusion that TV generally is not so free as other media. Mr. Mickelson noted that "most of the support which we at CBS news received when we were under fire in the Khrushchev issue came from newspapers, not from broadcasters." He said that "the press sets up a clamor when it is attacked. We have a tendency to sit back supinely until the storm blows itself out, and, in the meantime, hope that it will go away and leave us alone."[16]

Religious and educational institutions do not always provide commercial broadcasters with examples of courageous leadership in the treatment of controversial issues. Many a preacher and ecclesiastical executive is as fearful of offending his constituents as any operator of a radio or television station.

When the Metropolitan Educational Television Association of New York City produced a program, "The Faces of War," the New York Public Library ordered its name removed from the screen credits when a trustee feared that the presentation might be unwise pacifist propaganda, motivating Jack Gould to observe: "Much is heard about the timidity of commercial broadcasters and advertising in offering presentations that invite conflicting opinions. But very little is heard about quasi-public institutions, foundation groups and educational organizations that ostentatiously don the mantle of enlightened culture and then dash into cover at the first hint of stormy weather."[17]

News: Politics

One particular aspect of news coverage which offers unusual opportunities and pitfalls is the political scene. Here, indeed, the media may conceivably elevate man or degrade him, inform or delude him. Through political broadcasting is man developing into a more responsible citizen, or is he becoming a voting machine which is less-than-man?

Early in the history of broadcasting, politicians learned to respect the media. A 1932 story in *The Nation* tells how, at 8:30 P.M. one evening in that year, Herbert Hoover began a speech from Iowa. At 9:30, when Ed Wynn was expected, Hoover had reached only number two of a twelve-point program and thousands of votes shifted to Roosevelt. At 9:45, with Hoover only at his fourth point, two million switched off their radios and sent the children to bed weeping as more votes shifted. At 10 P.M. Hoover reached point seven, but ten million husbands and wives retired. Sixty stations received six thousand calls of protest.[18]

No modern political candidate would make such a mistake. He would hire media specialists to choose the issues, tell him what to say and how to say it, and control the image of himself which would reach the public. But in terms of man's capabilities and society's needs can this not lead to a much more crucial mistake? Our constitutional system rests upon the expectation that issues and candidates will be evaluated thoughtfully in the marketplace of ideas.

In contrast, Richard Nixon is said to have told the TV and Radio Executives Club of New York that "the public buys names and faces and not platforms" and that "a candidate for public office has to be merchandised in much the same way as any TV product."[19] If this includes the customary emphasis on oversimplified or fictitious distinctions among products it can tend to degrade the voters by offering delusively simple answers for complex but potentially understandable problems. This can and does lead to the substitution of spot announcements, soap-opera-like dramatizations and stage-managed political spectaculars for information and discussion. In the coverage of the national conventions microphones and cameras are lavishly deployed to convey a maximum of excitement and spectacle, often at the expense of meaningful information.

It must be admitted that pre-television days in politics were also something less than ideal. Bosses have been as influential as media experts in molding candidates; slogans such as "Tippecanoe and Tyler Too" fell short of enlightening the electorate on basic issues. But the mass media appear to be capable of helping the marketplace of ideas to function more effectively, thus contributing to man's growth, and there is a haunting question as to whether this potentiality is being realized or abused. Once again the question must be directed not only to broadcasters but to politicians and to voters. All three groups are represented in the churches where the question is infrequently asked.

Entertainment

The bulk of broadcasting is entertainment. Radio and television are the most conspicuous modern incarnations of show business. This is the emphasis in programing; this is the expectation of most listeners and viewers when they turn to their sets. At all hours of the day and night a flick of the switch can bring song or dance, laughter or tears into the living room, kitchen, or car. Many forms of orchestral and vocal music, drama, and variety can be brought to localities where, only a short lifetime ago, there was little but an occasional vaudeville show.

The overwhelming majority of Americans accepts this opportunity without criticism; a vocal minority rejects it without appreciation. Between the two viewpoints is an almost uncharted no-man's land where a few thoughtful people are wandering. This is the wilderness where the modern Christian is called to undertake a pilgrimage, realizing that he will be under fire from both directions, but knowing that he must express his point of view.

To an articulate minority the entertainment side of broadcasting is hopelessly degrading. Unlike "high culture" this "mass culture" is not the authentic creation of an individual artist and unlike genuine folk art it is not a spontaneous expression of the common people themselves. Instead it is a mass-produced, homogenized gruel intended only to anesthetize prospective customers for an operation on their purses. Its appeal is narcotic; its end is slavery. Ernest Van den Haag summarizes this view:

> All mass media in the end alienate people from personal experience and, though appearing to offset it, intensify their moral isolation from each other, from reality and from themselves . . . mass media, once they become a

habit, impair the capacity for meaningful experience . . . the habit feeds on itself, establishing a vicious circle as addictions do.[20]

It is also claimed that the mass media gradually destroy both "high culture" and folk art by monopolizing both artists and audiences. An artist either succumbs to the temptations of money and prestige offered by the media or despairs of reaching an appreciative audience and is driven into esoteric and nihilistic channels.

Defenders of broadcasting could reply that such a view is more guilty than the media of homogenization. It disregards great differences among programs, along with such phenomena as the sale of classical-music recordings, and holds out no hope for audiences to develop listening-viewing habits based on discriminating preferences. However, media enthusiasts are unlikely to have standards for entertainment other than the measurement of millions who tune to the programs. What is happening to them as they listen? What would they watch if they had the chance? Someone must take responsibility for asking such questions.

A Christian's analysis of entertainment cannot reflect only a concern for art in the sense of being "arty" or merely an interest in what is popular for the sake of popularity. Here, as with advertising and news, the Christian asks whether the listener-viewer is treated as man or less-than-man. This is not intended to look upon entertainment as propaganda or an exercise in didacticism; instead, the approach should coincide with the artists' own concern for integrity and authenticity.

The best of entertainment should stimulate the listener-viewer to respond with interrelated thoughts and feelings in ways which express and enlarge his humanity. He will participate through his imagination in an experience which will be truly recreative.

Entertainment: Dramatic Integrity

Great drama can provide the experience of purgation. It can deepen a person's understanding of life either by portraying reality or by rearranging reality in imaginative, creative forms. Many television dramas have portrayed man's needs, frustrations, and dilemmas with a clarity and profundity seldom achieved in any pulpit.

Recently, however, there has been a trend toward cancellation of the series which features such drama in favor of more programs with stereotyped plots and caricatures instead of characters. Within two seasons PHILCO, GOODYEAR, and KRAFT playhouses, STUDIO ONE, CLIMAX, MATINEE THEATER and ROBERT MONTGOMERY PRESENTS all disappeared from the air while soap operas and situation-comedies multiplied. (George Burns is credited with the definition of a situation-comedy as a play with a little more plot than a movie and a little less than a wrestling match.) Programs which use only a loose dramatic form but are unconcerned with authentic characterization and plot restrict the experience of the imagination and thus retard the development of the individual listener-viewer.

This danger is most apparent in the inevitable "happy endings" which oversimplify the problem of good and evil. Thus in one episode of MY FRIEND FLICKA the young hero conceals from his parents his knowledge of the identity of a murderer because his horse is being held as a hostage. A preposterous resolution is achieved when the boy captures the murderer because the horse, Flicka, has knocked him helpless.

Similarly, in one episode of LASSIE, young Jeff is so con-

cerned about two pigeons newly hatched in a nest block-
ing the barn door that he does not want his grandfather
to disturb them by rolling out a mowing machine needed
to cut ten acres of alfalfa in anticipation of a predicted
storm. After Jeff discusses the situation with his mother,
applying the Golden Rule to the pigeons, she convinces
the grandfather to risk the alfalfa because "the boy's
faith is at stake." During the night the storm comes as
expected, but a neighbor has cut the alfalfa before dark
without telling anyone! The "faith" at stake was evidently a superstitious belief that "everything would come
out all right" no matter how irresponsibly and stupidly
one acted.

It is not only in children's dramatic programs that the
dimension of reality may be overlooked. In "One Left
Over" on PLAYHOUSE OF STARS a man loses his wife and two
sons in an auto accident. Only he and a daughter remain
alive. In his sorrow he is plausibly perplexed by such
questions as: why did this happen to me? why couldn't
I have been killed too? However, before the audience
can be disturbed by any sensible thoughts three sensational elements are introduced: the father finds some sleeping
pills and considers suicide, he decides to postpone breaking the news of the accident to his daughter until the next
day, and a neighbor, even before the funeral, arranges
for the representative of a service agency to visit him to
discuss the possibility of placing the daughter in a foster
home. The situation is "resolved" when a neighboring
grandmother moves in to help carry on the home, causing
the man to say (with his wife and sons still unburied),
"The Lord giveth; the Lord taketh away. In this case, the
Lord taketh away, the Lord giveth!" A cynic could be
excused for retitling the play, "One Too Many Left Over."

77

On another occasion, in a radio series, a scripture passage was incorporated in a climactic scene when the Lone Ranger, attending a funeral, heard a clergyman read, "I am the resurrection and the life. He that believeth in me, though he were dead, yet shall he live." These words inspired the Lone Ranger to uncover a case of mistaken identity and prove that the corpse in the coffin was not the body of the person whose funeral was supposedly being held.

It is sobering in these instances to realize that many well-meaning churchgoers will welcome any such inclusion of a biblical quotation without recognizing how it is being prostituted. It is even more dreadful to realize that the scriptwriters could have been following the examples of some preachers whose sermons make similarly irrelevant use of biblical passages to offer quick and easy solutions to all problems. Still another blow to ecclesiastical smugness should come from the admission that nothing on radio or television is more implausible and degrading than much church-basement drama.

Broadcasting executives explain the decline in the number of high-quality dramatic series partly in terms of cost but also in terms of the scarcity of excellent scripts. The appetite of the media is enormous. A play which runs for hundreds of performances on Broadway is seen only once on television. A comedian could have played for a year in vaudeville with the material consumed on one program. It seems reasonable, then, to argue that there are simply not enough first-rate scripts to go around.

Entertainment: Escape and Escapism

Many writers and performers, however, reply that good scripts would be forthcoming if the industry encouraged them. Charles Boyer has said, "The agency has approval rights over stories and repeatedly rejects the best stories offered, so eventually we do feeble ones. There are so many taboos . . . a story is too violent, too daring, too morbid or too controversial . . . we are disheartened when we try our best for quality and they go for the corny stories."[21] One example of the reticence of the media to treat current issues dramatically is avoidance of the Negro-white integration problem in network dramatic scripts. Reginald Rose in "Thunder on Sycamore Street" and Rod Serling in "A Town Has Turned to Dust" had to change basic plot situations involving race relations to secure sponsor approval. This is one other area where it must be said that radio and television are no more cautious and timid than many other elements in society. To say this, however, should not be to abdicate responsibility for preserving mass communication channels for artists who want to do more than offer tranquilizers to help man forget his problems, who want to penetrate to the essentials of reality and help man to confront his predicament. In industry circles it is often remarked that one of the most heartbreaking aspects of television is the number of truly talented people who are frustrated and rotting.

The same thing is said regularly with respect to every artistic medium, but the problem is intensified in broadcasting where the emphasis is not simply on a "hit" but on a "smash hit," not simply on a box office of thousands but one of millions, not simply on millions but on *more* millions than can possibly be attracted by any competition regardless of its type of appeal. A related suspicion has been voiced by Gilbert Seldes: ". . . the whole entertainment side of broadcasting which surrounds its communication of ideas tends to create a mood of consent and acceptance; it cannot afford to stir and agitate the mind. . . . The broadcaster must paralyze the critical, questioning faculties of the human mind."[22]

But what can we expect of entertainment? Longhair critics of broadcasting compare its output with their own sources of recreation such as the best of foreign films, the Museum of Modern Art, and *Saturday Review*. For most listener-viewers more likely alternatives are pulp magazines and juke-boxes. If we adopt a standard which expects drama, comedy, and variety to develop man in some respect are we not confusing entertainment with education?

Surely nothing in these pages has suggested that entertainment must conform to the common practices of formal education in the systematic, sequential transmission of information. Indeed, formal education can sometimes profit by applying some of the principles of entertainment to the communication process. Nor have we meant to imply that entertainment must always be solemn and profound. The strains of living in the twentieth century create demands for relaxation; there is a place for escape which does not become escapism. The increased leisure available to most workers provides time for enjoyment of entertainment which can relieve tensions, anxieties, and loneliness, but which, like all art, can also speak to the meaninglessness of life. In many different ways it can contribute to the well-being of man without being accompanied by by-products which tend to make him less-than-man.

Appreciating the contribution of broadcast entertainment to life in twentieth-century America the Christian can nevertheless be alert for dehumanizing elements in programs.

Entertainment: Violence

Attention is often called to the prevalence of violence on the air, especially in children's programs. The quantity of these crimes has been documented in various monitoring studies. Psychologists and other students of the situation disagree concerning its effects. There is no reliable research demonstrating that such programs have harmed any but the most seriously maladjusted child. Most so-called juvenile delinquency is traceable to other, more immediate causes which could easily be overlooked if the mass media were publicized as the sole villain.

There is, however, a lurking suspicion that to be accurate we should say that there is not *yet* evidence of a *statistical* nature concerning harm done by crime programs. The long-range influence may not be measurable by currently available psychosociological instruments; but attention should also be given to the insights of artists, educators, and theologians concerning possible harm which may come from exposure to an imbalance of crime programs, especially if they involve unmotivated violence.

In view of the observable tendency of many listener-viewers to be uncritical about entertainment programs and to identify easily with the characters portrayed, the words of Walt Whitman have special significance: "There was a child went forth every day, and the first object he looked upon, that object he became, and that object became part of him for the day or a certain part of the day, or for many years or stretching cycles of years."[23]

The producers of crime programs frequently remind us that violence is not uncommon in some of the most highly respected literature, to which Edgar Dale replies, "The typical violent film or TV program . . . should not be compared with the use of violence by a great dramatist. I am not now suggesting that Shakespeare can get by with something that Mickey Spillane cannot. I simply ask: 'does the violence shown illuminate the wellsprings of conduct, help us better understand why people act the way they do?' Should bullets, guns, stabbing, kicking, abduction be the daily imagery of childhood?"[24]

Entertainment: Value and Image Portrayal

The influence of violence in programs may be less important than other elements. A government investigating committee in Great Britain exonerated gangster films from responsibility for juvenile delinquency but concluded that the movies' big danger is that they expose children "to the suggestion that the highest values in life are riches, power, luxury and public adulation, and that it does not matter very much how these are attained or used." The committee report continued: "We are convinced that the regular portrayal of false values is more persuasive and dangerous than the depiction of crime or impropriety."

In this country a group of people from television, psychology, and education conferred under the auspices of the Foundation for Character Education in association with Boston University and published a booklet, *Television for Children,* which suggests that "prolonged exposure" to Westerns and similar conflict dramas "makes children more stereotyped in their moral judgments— makes them more likely to see other people as 'all good' or 'all bad.'" The report goes on to say that since "conflict and choice characterize our society," children should be helped by TV to realize that there are various shades of good and bad instead of being exposed to "black-white, hero-villain concepts."[25]

Joseph Klapper has pointed out that television programs affect the images of adults which children form and that the discrepancy between the adults on TV and the adults known personally to the child creates bewilderment.

Do radio and television accustom a child to a heightened level of excitement which he soon demands all the time? Do they require increasingly stronger stimuli to offer new sensations? Do they reduce frustration tolerance by overexposure to situations too easily resolved? These subtler elements of influence within entertainment programs are probably the most significant, but not all the basic questions have yet been asked and few have been answered.

With adults as well as children the most significant levels of meaning in entertainment programs may be underneath the surface. What are the values exalted, the images conveyed, the attitudes assumed?

Both the public and the industry are quick to react to the false values suggested by "rigged" quiz programs, but even honestly conducted quizzes may place a false premium on the ability to recall inconsequential information, and giveaways may become opiates, inducing frustrated listener-viewers to flee from daily responsibilities into the dream of getting something fabulous for nothing.

Gilbert Seldes refers to STRIKE IT RICH and similar programs as "misery giveaways based on the idea that millions are so insecure that they need constant reassurance of the misery of others."[26]

On the program IT COULD BE YOU in the midst of a jolly interview a woman was shown and given a picture of her dead mother, giving millions the chance to watch her weep.

On PEOPLE ARE FUNNY a hypnotist influenced a man

from the audience to laugh stupidly no matter what happened to him or what was said to him. On the same program contestants telephoned ostensibly unknown persons and attempted (for $1,000) to prolong the conversation for three minutes. There was also an attempt to pair off unmarried people by an electronic computer, encouraging a romance and arranging for the couple to return weekly for reports.

In each of the cases above it is difficult to see how the studio and broadcast audiences could be regarded as men rather than less-than-men.

Entertainment: Subconscious Factors

Wilbur Schramm comments upon the prevalence in many programs of a surface moralism which makes everything come out all right in the end but which is basically dishonest by encouraging viewers to participate vicariously in crimes and illicit sex without any sense of guilt. He says:

> A criminal may be depicted as powerful, smart, successful, attractive, just so justice catches up with him at the end. All kinds of sexy and violent ideas may be written into popular art, provided we are told at the end that it was all a mistake; it didn't really happen. . . . I wonder whether the result is not . . . that everybody wallows in the filth and has a grand old time without any sense of moral guilt?[27]

It has been suggested that the typical soap opera reverses the role of psychiatry. Instead of drawing reality out of our subconscious it buries reality in our subconscious and encourages us to live in a dream world. This criticism does not imply that every program should be outright realism. In reaction to the 1959 quiz scandals there were many absurd suggestions, including one that the wires supporting Peter Pan in flight should be exposed to prevent deceit. Such a ridiculous proposal fails to distinguish between deceit and the artistic convention of illusion. It is one thing for a broadcast allegedly to report actuality, whether in terms of a quiz, special event, interview or laboratory test of a commercial product; it is still another for a drama to pretend to portray reality; and it is still another for a program to stir the imagination through fantasy. There is a place for fantasy, but it must be recognized as such. Fantasy confused with reality is potentially disruptive of personality.

A study being made under a grant from the Ford Foundation is observing the effects of motion pictures on persons facing problems. Viewers include some persons undergoing psychoanalysis and some not under analysis; films are chosen to fit the viewers' own problem areas. Dr. Arthur J. Brodbeck, working with Dr. Franz Alexander at Mt. Sinai Hospital, Beverly Hills, California, has reported, "Without being aware of it the fantasy gets into their dreams, their social relations, their moods. For the person in psychoanalysis, things can be speeded up. The conflict which has been in the subconscious is lifted up to the conscious quickly. . . . But if a person is not in analysis, it causes tremendous stress. Many get sick in bed with imaginary illness. Or they get depressed."[28]

Dr. Brodbeck maintains that when evaluative thought triumphs over emotion, fantasy dissolves. Thus listener-viewers may be immunized against the potentially harmful effects of such programs by developing the capacity to evaluate them.

85

Appreciation Possible

Is it unrealistic to hope for listener-viewers to learn to appreciate the better programs? In France a UNESCO study of television and rural adult education reported that the good taste revealed by unsophisticated viewers was "astonishing." Televised dramatic films were rated by audiences and although 90 per cent of the films shown were rated as bad by artists and critics, of seventeen favorites named by viewers only two or three were not masterpieces in the judgment of critics. There was also a great desire to see such telecasts again.

The same project studied reactions to informational programs and concluded that it is possible to interest ordinary audiences in important problems of public life. "Between a routine attitude to everyday existence, which cheapens its significance, and an escapist attitude, which denies it, there is room for a popular culture firmly linked to everyday work and leisure."[29]

Our glimpses into broadcasting advertising, news, and entertainment have been cursory rather than comprehensive. In suggesting the application of a standard (man or less-than-man) to various program elements we have encountered many uncertainties and complexities. Producers, sponsors, and listener-viewers would undoubtedly share the desire for more and more programs which serve man rather than debase him, which are worthy of the highest talents of writers and directors, the best efforts of performers, and the fullest response of audiences. How can this desire be fulfilled? At what points in our American system of broadcasting can steps be taken to encourage the best of programing? Again there are no easy answers but there are lines of direction which we shall explore in the next chapter.

CHAPTER 4

Prospects for Improvement

Radio and television are relatively new phenomena even in a young nation. Within the memory of one generation they have become pervasive forces in our society. Decisions concerning our national system have had to be made quickly. Is the resulting structure as satisfactory as it can be? Chapters 2 and 3 have demonstrated that the American broadcasting industry, like all other human institutions, has both strengths and weaknesses. Provision must be made to nourish the strengths and minimize the weaknesses. Is this being done, or could our present system be improved in various ways? Along with other democratic institutions the mass media should be subject to periodic re-examination.

Unlikely Alternative

There is little likelihood that the commercial industry which dominates the media in this country will be replaced by a public corporation, as in Great Britain. Comparatively few Americans are sufficiently dissatisfied with the existing system to favor a change which would require major support from taxation. We Americans have a traditional reluctance to pay for services through taxation; there is no comparable reluctance to allow business to incorporate the charge for services in the price of merchandise.

There is even a suspicion that the establishment of a public corporation for broadcasting would be out of line with our system of private enterprise. However, our schools are not operated on a profit-making basis, supported by advertising, nor is our postal system, and there would undoubtedly be widespread opposition to any such proposal for broadcasting.

Over a period of time broadcasting may be more influential than schools in the development of the individual and in the life of the nation. Is it reasonable that this medium for the communication of ideas should be administered by persons qualified primarily in show business or in merchandising? The British do not believe so, and the stated policies of the British Broadcasting Corporation reflect their conviction. A director-general of the BBC said, "The BBC's purpose is to be a source of information, education and entertainment, and a means of *raising* public taste. Not reflecting or ignoring it, but of raising it. That implies movement and progress."[1]

There is no evidence, however, that the BBC has been more successful than American radio and television in building audiences for quality programs. Burton Paulu's comprehensive study, *British Broadcasting,* concludes "that the standards of discrimination among listeners and viewers in the United Kingdom were no higher after thirty years of monopoly operation by the BBC than they were in the United States with its competitive system of broadcasting."[2] Mr. Paulu acknowledges that there may be many factors, other than broadcasting alone, which influence taste, but his observations undermine any claim that a monopolistic public corporation would be an easy answer to the problem of audience taste. Quality programs would not necessarily be more in demand.

As noted in the previous chapter, public operation of broadcasting would not necessarily improve the treatment of news and controversial issues. Quincy Howe has said, "In my four years as news analyst for Station WILL, operated as an outlet for educational radio by the University of Illinois, my freedom of expression was far more narrowly circumscribed than it ever has been on any commercial station or network." He expressed the opinion that this was a proper limitation for a tax-supported state university unwilling to offend any substantial group of its constituents and testified, "In my present capacity as news analyst for the American Broadcasting Network, I have never felt so free to speak my mind or had so much time in which to speak it."[3]

Religious broadcasters, both in this country and abroad, have also experienced greater freedom and flexibility in the use of commercial facilities than of public stations. Many American university and municipal stations are extremely restrictive in terms of religious broadcasting, and both Canadian and British churchmen have commented that private stations are frequently more receptive than public facilities to proposals for religious programs.

Supplemental Services

Although a monopolistic public broadcasting corporation does not appear to be a live option in the United States there is no reason why the commercial system cannot be supplemented by noncommercial operations. In Great Britain the BBC and commercial television now exist together, engaging in creative competition. In America there have always been radio stations operated by educational institutions and in recent years there has been a gradual but continual growth in the number of television stations operated by public organizations. There are several state educational broadcasting networks and one national tape network.

Most of the stations are noncommercial although the pioneer in television at Iowa State University sells time. Michigan State University shares time with a commercial broadcaster who pays a rental fee to the university. In some cities universities, public school systems, libraries, museums, and other organizations have united in the financing and operation of a station. Audiences generally are smaller than commercial station audiences but are far from insignificant. Like all public institutions the educational stations are sometimes susceptible to political pressures but in most respects they are not only free to serve minority tastes but may experiment and wait for tastes to develop. They supplement the broadcasting schedule in a community at the very points where commercial broadcasting is often weak. Many parts of the country, however, have no such station and there is need for increasing and strengthening the service. One of the pressing problems is the lack of Very High Frequency channels currently available for educational television.

Some commercial radio stations, especially FM outlets,

are also undertaking to serve minorities and thus balance the over-all media emphasis on the largest possible audiences at all times. In the larger cities especially, where even small minorities may number many thousands of people, this can be good business. With television holding the bulk of the audience for run-of-the-mill entertainment an alert radio station can attract listeners who want good music, informative discussion, or any one of many program elements not ordinarily available in the typical program schedule. Such an audience may be unusually valuable by commercial standards because it includes many persons not reached regularly by other programs. Here again, however, many parts of America enjoy no service of this kind.

Another possible supplementary program service is "Pay-TV" or subscription television, whereby broadcasters charge viewers for access to individual programs. Technically this is possible in one of various ways, but its advantages and disadvantages are the subject of a running debate. Proponents claim that this would freshen the media by introducing programs such as new motion pictures, great drama, and sporting events now economically impossible to present. It is also argued that more educational, artistic, and inspirational programs would be available to people willing to pay for them, although there might be some question as to whether enough people would pay. Opponents claim that the enormous potential box office would only intensify the conditions which now exist; that substantially the same programs would be offered, but that the viewers would be paying directly to see them. It is even suggested that the outcome might be *both* viewer-payment *and* commercials. This, of course, could be prevented by the regulations authorizing the establishment of the system. "Pay-TV" would probably supplement the present system in some respects, undoubtedly duplicate it in others.

Technical Limitation on Expansion

Educational broadcasting, commercial stations serving minorities, subscription television, all have possibilities for improving our American system by offering a greater diversity of programs. Handicapping any such development, however, is the technical limitation on the number of AM and VHF channels available in a particular area. Except for a few metropolitan areas FM channels are available for radio and UHF channels for television, but the limited number of FM and UHF sets in those same areas puts an intolerable burden on the broadcaster. He can get permission to go on the air, but he is unlikely to have many listener-viewers because few people are so dissatisfied with programs available on AM and VHF channels that they will pay to adapt their sets to receive a single new FM or UHF station. It is probably too late to do much about radio, except to encourage the continued growth of FM, but a more radical step is needed in television.

The Federal Communications Commission originally authorized television companies in this country to operate on the Very High Frequency band, or VHF. There are only twelve channels on this band and, to avoid interference, stations must be distributed according to population and geographical factors. Of the one hundred most densely populated communities in the United States only seven have a choice of four or more VHF stations; twenty-six have three, thirty-two have two, and nineteen only one.

In 1948 the FCC belatedly foresaw this congestion and

"froze" the granting of licenses until a study could be made. After a four-year delay the Ultra High Frequency band was opened to accommodate seventy channels. Meanwhile, however, seventeen million VHF sets had been purchased to receive 108 VHF stations operating in sixty-three communities. The broadcaster granted a UHF license, except in areas where no VHF station is operating, is almost hopelessly handicapped; and two-thirds of the channels allocated for educational television are in the UHF band.

If the UHF band could be utilized fully there would be room for the diversity of programing which could enrich American television. The FCC, however, is reluctant to move. Should all of television be moved to the UHF band? Should some areas be retained for VHF and their number of channels increased at the expense of other areas which would be converted totally to UHF? VHF broadcasters naturally defend the *status quo,* and set-owners are not happy at the prospect of having to purchase adapters.

It would be possible to shift gradually to UHF through a period of duplicate service while most present sets were being replaced through normal obsolescence if all new receivers were equipped for both VHF and UHF. However, competition among set manufacturers is keen, and if sets suitable for dual reception must be sold at a higher price, no maker is inclined to place its dealers and retailers under such a handicap unless UHF programs are generally available. One suggestion for breaking this vicious circle calls for a five-year exemption from the federal tax on television receivers able to pick up both VHF and UHF telecasts. Proponents state that the tax thus waived would offset the higher manufacturing cost and enable the maker to retain a competitive position. Legislation providing for such temporary exemption has failed to receive public support, while the vested interests in VHF equipment and licenses have naturally "viewed with alarm." To effect a gradual transition from the confines of VHF to the roominess of UHF, both the Congress and the FCC must be encouraged really to take hold of the problem and develop a practicable solution. Here is the opportunity for citizens to be helpfully vocal now.

A Purpose Beyond Profits

Even if accomplished, an increase in the number of channels being used in an area will not automatically increase the diversity of program offerings. A single station, responsibly operated, may offer greater program variety and quality than half a dozen stations imitating each other in scrambling for the same segment of the audience at all times. Achievement of creative and varied programing is ultimately dependent upon the enlightened policies of management.

Many American commercial broadcasters are fully aware of the weaknesses of much programing and would like to improve the situation. But where can they turn for active allies? Listener-viewers? Educational institutions? Sponsors? One thoughtful executive points out that there are many Christian laymen in the leadership of companies which buy radio and television time, who should recognize their responsibility along with the broadcaster. He writes:

"It is my belief that it is the Christian duty of every business man to operate his business, not for financial gain alone, but to be of service to the community also. While

I am not opposed to financial gain, I do not think it is enough.

"We have in the churches thousands of business men who are the top officials of companies which purchase radio and television advertising. What about exploring the field of the Christian layman raising standards in broadcasting by raising the type of program he will purchase to advertise his product or service? I am not trying to release the broadcasting people from their responsibilities."[4]

Others have proposed that industries become modern patrons of the arts by subsidizing such programs as great dramas, operas, and documentaries. Edward R. Murrow suggested that each of the twenty or thirty big corporations which dominate radio and television should "give up one or two of their regularly scheduled programs each year, turn the time over to the networks, and say in effect: 'This is a tiny tithe, just a little bit of our profits. On this particular night we aren't going to try to sell cigarettes or automobiles; this is merely a gesture to indicate our belief in the importance of ideas.'"[5] Such a project would probably still leave untouched some of the most crucial and controversial issues of our society because advertisers and their agencies would be reluctant to displease any segment of society, but the proposal holds such far-reaching possibilities that it merits consideration.

A more basic handicap to such proposals is the slowness of many broadcasters and advertisers to adopt a purpose other than the annual increase in net profits. Kenneth Bartlett, pioneer in broadcast education, has said, "After thirty years of attempting to prepare personnel for broadcasting, I still cannot feel genuine desire on the part of the broadcasting profession to acquire a transcendent aim, or, in fact, to seek personnel who have it."[6]

Other elements of American business are searching for such a transcendent aim. O. A. Ohmann of the Standard Oil Company of Ohio says:

> Certainly no people have ever had so much, and enjoyed so little real satisfaction. Our economy has been abundantly productive, our standard of living is at an all-time peak, and yet we are a tense, frustrated, and insecure people full of hostilities and anxieties. Can it be that our *god of production* has feet of clay? . . .
> There is nothing wrong with production but we should ask ourselves: *"Production for what?"* Do we use people for production or production for people? How can production be justified if it destroys personality and human values both in the process of its manufacture and by its end use?[7]

It is difficult to imagine how a radio or television station can truly serve "the public interest, convenience, and necessity" if the dominant purpose in the minds of owners and staff is the continual increase of profits by pandering to wants which may degrade rather than ennoble men. There is nothing in the American system which makes this inevitable, but if a more fundamental aim is to be recognized within the industry it must be articulated, advocated, and implemented. At this point Christian laymen in broadcasting have a vocational witness to make.

Development of Discrimination

If program offerings are somehow diversified there is still no guarantee of growth in discrimination on the part of listener-viewers. We have noted Burton Paulu's conclusion that thirty years of BBC did not make a significant difference in British tastes. Some would say that this is at least partly due to the fact that the more enlightening programs of the BBC have been stodgy and unpalatable, making no concession to the varying levels of intellect and sophistication among the audience. Beyond this, however, Mr. Paulu's conclusion reinforces earlier studies from this country indicating that mere exposure to better programs is not enough, that programs nourish the growth of taste only when a seed has already been planted. Audiences for classical music have grown in size, and radio—along with recording—nourished this growth; but analysis of individuals reveals that in most cases initial interest was stimulated by a companion or group of companions.

This is in line with the general conclusion that broadcasting contributes to the development of tastes and attitudes, but its influence cannot be isolated from other factors. Joseph Klapper says that the mass media function "among and through a nexus of mediating factors and influences."

If the media, by themselves, are so limited in their potentiality to elevate man, why are they pictured as so dangerous in their potentiality to degrade him? The answer is affected by a person's view of human nature, but the power of the media must neither be minimized nor exaggerated. Max Lerner puts it this way: "While in the long run the audience possesses a legislative power over its own tastes and ideas, there is at any time a frame of permissiveness within which the technicians of the Big-Audience media can work either creatively or destructively, either to degrade and corrupt what they find or to evoke its potential."[8]

The media can be influential within limits, but personal groups set the limits and even mediate influence within these limits. Some groups within education and religion which are quite vocal in complaining about the dangers of broadcasting are either unaware of their own responsibilities or unwilling to assume them. August Heckscher says, "A certain cussedness and obduracy in the individual is the best defense against the pressure of the mass media. Too many of our colleges simply reflect the marketplace, too many of our churches are saturated with its values."[9]

What is needed is not snobbish isolation from the media but the development of more discriminating listener-viewers. John Mason Brown has said, "People who deny themselves a television deny themselves participation in life today . . . they are self-exiled from the world. They suffer from the most painful illiteracy, which is that of the literate. In terms of reporting conversation, ideas or drama, television can do something that no other medium has done. And for the viewer the responsibility of self-editing, of selection, is the same as in choosing a book, a play or a motion picture. It becomes an exercise of will; a demonstration of taste."[10]

Responsibility of the Home

More professional critics can assist in the development of this discrimination. Newspapers and periodicals offer fewer thoughtful analyses of broadcasts than of dramas, concerts, and motion pictures. Ultimate responsibility, however, rests in the school, the church, and especially the home.

Television is sometimes acclaimed for its achievement in bringing the family back together in the home. Even within the limited accuracy of this claim it must be noted that there are restricted benefits to mere physical proximity. Group television viewing is not a social experience unless it is made so. Watching television may stifle conversation, but it also offers the *possibility* for the development of understandings and for thoughtful discussions. Alert parents can learn much about children from their responses to telecasts, and there is frequent opportunity for group consideration of issues which might not otherwise come to the surface. Children can also be helped to learn not only to discriminate against the worst programs but to develop powers of enjoying the better ones.

Potentially harmful influences commonly attributed to the media can usually be overcome in the home. Broadcasting is often accused of luring children away from the out-of-doors and from needed physical recreation. Studies show, however, that most children are easily attracted from radio and television by more active recreation which the family can make available. Communities, too, must remember that entertainment need not be confined to spectator-amusements and must provide recreational facilities for the increasing population.

Broadcasting is also accused of affecting reading habits adversely, but this is not at all inevitable. Research indicates that the reading of such material as comic books and popular fiction magazines is likely to be reduced in favor of television viewing, but some serious reading is stimulated by specific programs. Encouragement from the home can help broadcasting to promote rather than decrease reading. Parents who seldom do any serious reading themselves can hardly be surprised if the most questionable radio and television programs become obsessions for their children, but in homes where the best of books and magazines are shared by the family, reading is not likely to be crowded out by broadcasting. The terrorizing effect of some adventure programs is also minimized in the home where the child knows real affection and security.

Audience Response

Listener-viewers who develop appreciation for programs which serve man's real needs will want to encourage stations to carry more such programs. What can be done? Are there open channels of communication between broadcasters and the audience?

Surveys regularly estimate the size of audiences and will reflect major shifts in listening-viewing habits. They do not, however, predict what listener-viewers would select if given the chance. Mail is given serious consideration by station personnel, especially if it consists of individually written comments rather than form letters. Most programs receive little mail response. GUNSMOKE, with an audience averaging more than forty-seven million, draws an average of twenty-five letters per program. The DOUGLAS EDWARDS news program, with more than six million viewers, receives only about five letters per program. For this reason the opinions of letter writers are sometimes given an importance out of proportion to their actual numbers. It is not unusual for a local station, when considering a schedule revision, to keep a program on the air when as few as twenty-five persons write in favor of it.

In some communities there are committees attempting to express the desires of citizens to broadcasters. In Boston the Committee for Better Broadcasting analyzed the schedules of nine Boston radio stations and found that news reports and teen-tuned music occupied 81 per cent of daytime programing. The Committee charged that this showed "a complete lack of balance" in the schedules and said that programing should be geared more for "home-makers who constitute by far the greatest group of listeners during these daytime hours."[11]

Consultative Commissions

A few stations have their own consultative committees composed of citizens from their coverage areas. Radio station WTTM, in Trenton, New Jersey, has a Community Program Committee consisting of fifty-five representatives from education, religion, industry, government, and civic organizations. The full committee meets twice a year but an executive board meets monthly with the station manager, program director, and news director.

Various individuals and groups have proposed a national citizens' advisory commission to represent the public in consultations with the industry. The Commission on Freedom of the Press recommended the establishment of a "new and independent agency to appraise and report annually" upon the performance of the mass media. The proposal called for a board of distinguished citizens and a competent staff to undertake such services as the following:

- Helping the media "define workable standards of performance";
- "Pointing out the inadequacy" of media service in certain areas;
- Investigating areas and instances "where minority groups are excluded from reasonable access to the channels of communication";

- Investigating charges of deceptive reporting, with particular reference to misrepresentation of the data required for judging public issues;
- Appraising "governmental action affecting communications";
- Encouraging projects which give hope of meeting the needs of special audiences;
- Giving "the widest possible publicity and public discussion to all its findings."[12]

If such an agency is ever to be established, an independent group of people must take the initiative. This is not the task of either government or the media, although the agency should counsel with both. The churches could undertake at least to promote consideration of this proposal by the public.

In theory, of course, the public is already sufficiently represented in relationship to broadcasting by the Federal Communications Commission. As noted earlier in these pages, however, the stand taken by the Commission with respect to programing has been neither strong nor clear.

Canada's Royal Commission on Broadcasting recently attempted to deal with a similar situation in that country. The report recommended that private radio and television stations be recognized as a permanent feature of Canadian broadcasting but added:

"This is not to say that any individual private operator has any vested interest which entitles him, as of right, to continue in existence. Each private operator, as the holder of a valuable, temporary right to use a relatively rare public asset, should justify the continued retention of that right—and should be required to keep on justifying it." The report noted that in the past, once a license was granted to a private operator, there was little control over his performance. It was recommended, instead, that "in future the standards of performance of private stations should be more effectively checked, that those who give inadequate public service or shabby performances under their franchises should be warned, and that the licenses of those who fail to make improvements after such warnings should be cancelled."[13]

There is a similar need in this country for a strengthening, or at least a clarification, of the responsibility and authority of the Federal Communications Commission. If the FCC actively exercises the functions originally intended for it there may be no need for a citizens' advisory commission. If, on the other hand, it is concluded that it is unhealthy in a democracy to assign the review of programing to a governmental agency, some sort of independent commission is essential.

At present, we have neither an effective FCC nor an alternative in the form of a consultative commission on behalf of the public. As a result the industry is probably subject to more violent criticism than if certain checks and balances were operating. John Fischer, editor-in-chief of *Harper's* Magazine, has made a drastic proposal. He suggests that 10 to 15 per cent of every station's earnings—which would amount nationally to fifty million dollars or more—be charged for their use of the air and that this money be used to produce perhaps six hour-long public service programs a week. The stations would also be required to surrender prime evening time for the programs which would be produced by a National Broadcasting Authority, chartered by Congress. Programs would involve news-in-depth, top-quality music and theater, documentaries dealing with science, the arts and public affairs, and experimental features.[14]

Such a proposal has many weaknesses and little chance of being adopted, but it does reflect a growing conviction that an industry which uses public property to exist and which exerts social influence beyond present measurement must devise means by which the motive of private profit and the needs of the public are kept in some sort of balance, no matter how uneasy. It is important for the industry to respond to outside demands for constructive programing, but it would be even better if more such attempts were initiated from within.

Broadcasters, remembering that they are legally responsible to the FCC, must also retain actual control over their programs and not abdicate to advertising agencies and sponsors. Failure in this respect would provide cause for the Commission to consider prohibiting sponsorship of *programs*, allowing commercial interests to buy only the time actually devoted to *advertising*, as is the case in British commercial television. It must be recognized, however, that this practice could raise economic problems, especially at first. To compensate for the loss of revenue from the sale of blocks of time, stations and networks would have to charge much higher rates for spot announcements or multiply the number of announcements carried. In Britain it is not unusual at night to see six consecutive commercial announcements between programs, or even during breaks within programs.

One weakness of the existing system is unquestionably the ignorance of the public concerning its own rights and responsibilities. We noted that the Federal Communications Commission is under great pressures from industry and government, but that listener-viewers are notoriously silent. At the very least, citizens could express themselves in support of or in opposition to a particular station's type of operation when its license is up for renewal.

Ideally, such a representation before the Commission would not come as a surprise to the station because the individual or group would have communicated regularly with the station's executives. Protestants, of course, will not enter into any such relationship with the intention of exercising censorship. The expression of praise and censure, however, is a legitimate function of a group with a heritage of testifying, reforming, protesting, and proclaiming.

The industry needs assistance in developing its own professional standards and sense of social responsibility. The defects of the mass media are not greatly different from the weaknesses of other contemporary institutions, but the media lack an internal corrective force characteristic of those institutions. In government there is always the opposition party to point out the errors of incumbents; in schools there are parents and insurgent educational philosophers to scrutinize policies and practices; in churches the biblical tradition nurtures occasional prophets to fan the refining fires. Not that the path of genuine reformation is ever a smooth one in government, church, or school, but there is even less provision for corrective voices to be heard in the broadcasting industry.

In the heyday of big-money quiz programs there was more than a suspicion within the industry that they were not the genuine contests they pretended to be. In one way or another, with or without the consent of contestants, many of the programs were manipulated to provide suspense and sensation. And why not? By accepted industry standards they were very successful; look at the ratings they achieved! What if they involved a certain amount of deceit? Was it so different from the deceit in some other programs and advertising? After all, it was not illegal! It was not even any more immoral than the forms of deceit constantly practiced by countless Americans—including church members—in many phases of daily life.

So there was no active opposition until the deceit was exposed and a furore arose. Then executives made pious pronouncements, and producers were fired for the sake of appearances. The pressure, however, had come from outside the industry instead of from within. Instead of engaging in critical self-examination when questions are raised concerning its sense of responsibility, the industry is more likely to vote a budget for a public relations drive to convince the public that everything is really all right after all.

The fuss over such problems as the quiz programs should not be allowed to overshadow the need for consultation on more basic issues. What the industry is doing badly is probably less significant than what the industry is failing to do. It is at this point that Christians should be able to provide constructive assistance if given the opportunity.

Thoughtful Christians will also see the mass media in relation to all other elements in society. They will realize that broadcasting is neither a glamorous wonder-worker nor a villainous scapegoat. They will realize that attitudes and morals are not determined by any single medium, not even a mass medium, and that the alleged dangers of certain broadcasts must not be allowed to divert attention from the responsibilities of the home, the school, recreational agencies, the law-enforcement system—and the church, whose special opportunities and problems we are about to examine.

CHAPTER **5**

The Church's Task of Communication

We have waited until now to consider religious broadcasts because they are so few and their influence so meager in comparison with other programs on the daily schedule of most stations. The scarcity of religious broadcasts may be a symbol of a prevalent American attitude. Networks and many stations tend to crowd their few religious broadcasts into Sunday morning, reinforcing the twisted idea that religion is something to which attention should be given for one hour weekly.

In fairness to the stations it must be added that the quality of most religious broadcasts has not encouraged program executives to add to their number. On the whole,

108

churches have not taken their broadcasting opportunities seriously. To some extent this is due to apathy and lethargy. There are thoughtful churchmen, however, who question seriously the value of the mass media in the service of the church. The fact that radio and television are pervasive sources of entertainment and advertising, does not necessarily qualify them for other purposes. Are they appropriate instruments for employment by the churches?

It is generally agreed that the central task of the church is communication, but this does not automatically justify the use of the mass media. The theory of relativity can be communicated and so can the mumps, but radio and television are not effective media for either purpose. Is the Christian gospel so specialized, so rarified that a mass medium is inappropriate for its transmission? Is the Christian faith so private, so intimate that a mass medium is incapable of transmitting it? The nature of Christian communication must be examined before the mass media can be evaluated as possible instruments.

The Word at Work in the World

A commission appointed by the United Church of Canada to study its relationship to broadcasting declared that the church exists to proclaim "the good news that God has come to share our human lot in the life, death, and resurrection of Christ for the purpose of redemption and reconciliation. This is the Word, without reference to which no other fact or concern of life can be properly understood."[1] This is admittedly a technical statement of something so profound as to defy verbal description; in its present form it probably has meaning only for persons already within the community of believers. Yet it is not intended to be restricted to them. Instead, it suggests that something has happened which is so important as to change all of life and that whoever knows about this is enlisted to transmit its significance to everyone else.

To attempt this is not easy. Genuine *communication* between persons requires finding something held in *common* to serve as a bridge. When both persons are within a single *community* the task should not be too difficult. When, however, communication is attempted between persons coming from different backgrounds there must be a search for words, symbols, or images that will be mutually understandable. Beyond this there must be a reaching out in love for a relationship that will give meaning to words which would otherwise never become clear. Indeed, the full meaning of many Christian terms can never be grasped except from within the community of believers.

We cannot, however, allow the complexity of the communication process to discourage us from engaging in it. The attempt must begin somewhere and must take some form. The Christian believes that in Christ a mysterious God has communicated himself in terms at least partly comprehensible to man. "The Word was made flesh, and dwelt among us, and we beheld his glory, the glory as of the only begotten of the Father, full of grace and truth." Following Him we are called to communicate the clear and living Word at work in the world. This is both our burden and our joy. If we ponder it and stand under its judgment we may also proclaim the Word to others.

This Word is much more than an idea or a proposition; it is a perpetual event which began with the story of Israel and continues with the Christian church. As the expression of a living relationship it goes far beyond words. A child learns to know the love of parents before words are understood, and the deepest of human emotions are seldom expressed adequately through words alone. The Word in the world is not confined to what is spoken and written, but includes what is demonstrated, lived, and artistically created.

Relevance Without Conformity

Since eventually we must raise the question as to what extent radio and television are possible vehicles for the transmission of the Word in the world, attention should be called to the nature of the Word as news. Although the Word is not derived from man's nature or situation it speaks relevantly to that situation because it is spoken by the Creator of man and his world. It does not consist of ethereal abstractions, but it says something which makes a vital difference in every aspect of life, contrary to the impression often given by the Christian community that it is an esoteric cult conversing in technical language about things totally unrelated to the world.

Persons who shy away from religious broadcasting on the incredible grounds that the Gospel makes rather dull listening-viewing have no understanding of the vitality of the Word. The news of God's breaking into history may be unbelievable, offensive, and demanding, but never dull. Only the dilutions and substitutes are dull.

In biblical history the Word was given to a specific situation and addressed to a particular people. So today the Word must meet the particularity of the human situation. In our generation we have influential allies in artists and scholars who alert man to his anxieties, frustration, lostness, aloneness, and meaninglessness. Persons who do not consciously admit a sense of deep need are unconsciously avoiding that very admission. If the Word is spoken with any clarity whatever, it should be possible for some hearers to perceive its relevance to fundamental human needs.

The church must remember, then, that it is in the world. "As thou hast sent me into the world, so I have sent them into the world." But at the same time it must not be forgotten that the church is not "of the world." "They are not of the world, even as I am not of the world." In a world where radio and television are suspected of encouraging trends toward conformism Paul's warning is especially contemporaneous, "Do not be conformed to this world, but be transformed by the renewal of your mind." It is all right to meet listener-viewers where they are, but it is hardly worthy of a Christian broadcast simply to leave them there. The emphasis on relevance must not become simply an accommodation to man's situation, reducing the Word to a psychological or sociological panacea. Christian communication should deal not only with questions people are asking but with questions they should be asking and will ask if given a little stimulation.

The thoughtless churchman entering the unfamiliar, mysterious world of broadcasting may adopt uncritically the approach of some advertisers. He asks what the listener-viewers want and then makes whatever claims are necessary on behalf of the church to supply that want. Thus he sprinkles a little holy water on the technique of winning friends and influencing people. David Read remarks, "The preacher who is sensitive to the public pulse at any given moment is always under the temptation of responding to a popular demand rather than demanding a popular response. In other words, he is eliciting, probably unconsciously, his message from those to whom he speaks, rather than witnessing to the truth of the entrusted message."[2]

Joseph Sittler has articulated the double character of Christian communication in terms of three familiar concepts:

"*Faith* is related to man's nature and his need; but if presented as simply engendered by nature and need, and not as a faith in the faithfulness of God, that is, as trust in its object, it is distorted into a psychological reassurance or degraded into some sort of bonding agent which can then be exploited as a necessary civil glue for the life of the Republic.

"*Love* is related to man's nature and need; but if presented simply as a free-flowing human resource itself in no need of the fires of redemption, it becomes a name for the most adored illusion ever to seduce mankind. Christian love is born not simply of love itself, as expanded, sensitized or even cauterized by suffering, but out of the love wherewith we are beloved.

"*Hope* in the Christian understanding is not simply resolute hopefulness. It is a 'living hope' to which men have to be 'born again.' Its source is not in a religiously informed and optimistic reading of history or in the solitary human career as this may be temperamentally disposed toward the bright side of things; its source is again its Object, the 'God of Hope' who, we pray, may 'grant us joy and peace in believing.' "[3]

Only this double character of the Christian faith and the Christian life can make sense of the strange speech of the New Testament. The world is there called our proper place of obedience, the place where we are called

113

to "go and do likewise"—the theater in which Christ is to be obeyed by service to "the least of these, my brethren." But this same world is called "no abiding city," a place of pilgrimage. It is given us as our house precisely on the ground that it does not become our home. Every historic confession of Christendom has stressed this double character of the Christian hope.

Criterion: Faithfulness

How can this two-sided nature of Christian communication be maintained? Hendrik Kraemer suggests that faithfulness is a more valid criterion than success: "The best communication does not necessarily guarantee success. The search for successful communication has no Biblical justification. Only the search for faithful, really interpretative communication has."[4]

Not everyone will find the Word interesting, meaningful, and convincing, even when it is expressed most forcefully. This, however, is no justification for lazy and shoddy attempts at communication. As Paul Tillich puts it:

> There is always a genuine decision against the Gospel for those for whom it is a stumbling block. But this decision should not be dependent on the wrong stumbling block, namely, the wrong way of our communication of the Gospel—our inability to communicate. What we have to do is to overcome the wrong stumbling block in order to bring people face to face with the right stumbling block, and to enable them to make a genuine decision.[5]

The de-emphasis on success, then, does not excuse a lapse into obscurantism, nor does it imply an unconcern for the persons with whom we are attempting to communicate. It lets the question of ultimate "success" rest with God, knowing that immediate "success" and "failures" may be reversed in time, but it places squarely upon us the responsibility for transmitting as faithfully as possible what has been entrusted to us. This faithfulness to the Word demands a relevance which is entirely different from conformity or accommodation. The Christian broadcaster is not required to be popular, but he is required, like all other Christians, to be faithful, hopeful, loving, and honest. In his vocation as broadcaster he must also be interesting, challenging, provocative, and competent at communicating essential ideas as well as a sense of basic integrity in his work and person.

Communication en Masse?

In the proclamation of this two-edged Word do the mass media have a contribution to make? Certain limitations are obvious.

The term, "mass," itself raises disturbing questions. Can the Gospel be communicated en masse? Isn't there something basically incongruous in an attempt to establish or even discuss the personal, intimate divine-human relationship through a medium which attracts millions for a single program? What happens to the "fellowship of the redeemed" when the listeners to a proclamation cannot be seen by or respond directly to the proclaimer?

Of course there were times when Jesus spoke to thousands, and when Peter preached on Pentecost three thousand persons were baptized. We do not know how many of those three thousand remained faithful or how many of them had been prepared by previous, close association with our Lord and his followers, but we do know that Jesus and the early apostles customarily worked with individuals and small groups where questions and dialogue

115

were possible. The apostles had a continuing opportunity to articulate their doubts, their fears, and their misunderstandings as they lived and traveled with their Teacher. The fact that they denied and betrayed him makes it eternally and desperately clear that the most intimate acquaintanceship with him is not too much! How, then, can we expect vast, impersonal, one-way media to bring men and women to him? Can the mass media really deal with individuals?

In a superficial way, of course, they can. People are not listening to the radio or watching television in large gatherings; most of them are watching and listening alone or in family groups. Familiar personalities come through the air into the home with such regularity and calculated intimacy that they are often regarded as the closest of friends. This, however, is not so much a genuine, personal relationship as a synthetic "togetherness."

Recognizing this possible limitation does not necessarily discredit the usefulness of the media but may narrow the function somewhat. It may also help to make clear that in employment of the media the church cannot abdicate her own essential responsibility for the continuing engagement of two-way communication. Instead of replacing other functions of the church, broadcasting should stimulate and extend them. Unfortunately, the preaching and teaching activities of the local congregation are sometimes no better than the mass media in encouraging participation and "feedback."

Commercial Influences

From the Christian perspective another limiting characteristic of the mass media in this country is their commercial orientation. This is not to accuse anyone of insidious motives; it is simply to acknowledge the involvement of both the media and the church in contemporary culture. The clergyman who finds himself devoting more attention to a mortgage than a message is already tempted to twist the Word into a utilitarian commodity, and the mass media enlarge this temptation. The religious broadcaster is under pressures to oversimplify, to banalize, and to moralize.

Broadcasting, especially radio, calls for shorter and shorter programs. What was fifteen minutes in length becomes five and what was five becomes one. We have noted the concern of serious journalists with this trend. When the "good news" is compressed into a capsule it is usually transformed into just another pink pill. It is true that many religious broadcasts as well as sermons could be improved by judicious cutting, but this is often because the program or preacher has little to say anyway.

Occasionally a person may take a minute or less to express an idea which is striking, provocative, and even profound, as in Reinhold Niebuhr's frequently quoted prayer, "O God, grant me the serenity to accept the things I cannot change; give me the courage to change what should be changed, and the wisdom to distinguish the one from the other." Lincoln's conciseness also comes to mind, but few contemporary broadcasters will claim to match Lincoln's linguistic ability; and it is unlikely that Lincoln himself would have been able and willing to formulate classic statements to meet stop-watch specifications. A single, simple idea may be expressed in a very brief statement, but a more comprehensive idea should not be so cramped, lest it be mutilated and deformed. Confining religious broadcasts to "simple" ideas could lead to complete distortion of the Word.

The commercial emphasis on audience size may influence artistic factors such as the choice of music for a broadcast. Melodies and arrangements may be selected solely because of their popular appeal without regard for their secular association or the nature of the emotions aroused by them. The sentimentality of many a "religious pops" tune often contradicts the verbal content of the rest of the program.

We have observed the prevalence of "happy endings" in broadcasting, a contagion to which religious communicators are notably susceptible. Both in sermons and in drama the climactic sections may be unrelated to the earlier portions, or at least the resolutions often fail to follow from the given circumstances. Contrary to the sharp realism of the authentic Word, Christian broadcasts often evade the hard issues of life. Churchmen can be at least as guilty as commercial broadcasters of deceptive oversimplification.

Bishop Gerald Kennedy has said bluntly, "Too much of our television efforts have all the banality of a soap opera." He acknowledges that soap opera viewers need a healing ministry but maintains, "If you heal them on the soap opera level, you heal them too lightly, which is to say, you do not heal them at all. . . . This kind of presentation becomes a part of the disease, and not a part of the healing. . . . It puts religion in the same category with Tums, Bufferin and Lucky Strikes."[6]

If a minister were invited to present a five-minute portion of a nightclub floor show he would give careful thought to the question of whether or not to accept and if he did so he would struggle painfully with the decision as to how best to use those five minutes. Similarly the church must ask the delicate question concerning the degree to which the context of broadcasting transforms content and then decide whether what is left is sufficiently recognizable as Christian to justify the effort.

Participation Without Capitulation

We shall never know whether the effort is justified until we have tried a more courageous and thoughtful approach to religious broadcasting than has yet been attempted. There are formidable handicaps facing the church in using the media but we shall discover whether these handicaps can be overcome only by plunging into the world of radio-television and finding out.

Persons who are both ignorant of broadcasting and unreasonably afraid of it seize upon its limitations as sufficient excuse for having nothing to do with it, but this is unworthy of the church. In every mission situation, whether in lands where Christianity has never before been known or in inner-city parishes where it has long been disregarded, missionaries testify to the importance of participating fully in the situation within which they are working. They must live with the people in their area, understand them, and accept them—and be accepted by them—before it is possible to become agents for their redemption. Persons who want to be used for God's purposes of reconciliation must be willing to get soiled or injured in the process. We recognize this necessity in such obvious forms of crossbearing as risking infection and the persecution of hostile governments, but we are less aware of the need to suffer esthetically in the struggle to achieve genuine communication. Subtle but very real sacrifices are demanded of the religious broadcaster who attempts to understand and get through to the person who is captivated by the most degrading programs of the mass media. The church in the world of radio-television must recognize its mission to cultural delinquents.

This does not mean that the church must capitulate to the standards of the world of broadcasting. We need not simply copy the programs which have the greatest mass appeal. On every missionary frontier there is always the question as to how much of an indigenous culture may be respected and retained and how much should be revised and redeemed. The church *in* the world of television cannot be *of* that world, lest its distinctive nature be perverted.

But neither must the church stay out of the world of the mass media in order to remain true to its purposes.

The attempt to present the Word in a form which will enable its relevance to be recognized by more people does not necessarily lead to distortion. The person who tries most intently to interpret and translate a message usually discovers that his own understanding of the message is deepened. Every teacher and parent has been driven to a fresh examination of his ideas in the process of expounding them to students and children. To translate the Word for purposes of communication is altogether different from popularizing it. Paul, who strove to be "all things to all people," saw most clearly that the Gospel will often be offensive because it not only comforts the afflicted but afflicts the comfortable. Participating in the world does not mean capitulating to it by adapting the Word to the world's desires and demands. Participation calls for discrimination and persistent faithfulness in the face of misunderstanding and even opposition.

Now it is time to see what happens when the church attempts to participate in the world of radio-television, when the Word comes into this particular world. What emerges in terms of broadcasts? This will be our next field of investigation.

CHAPTER **6**

The Scope of Christian Broadcasts

The Word which the church is called to speak to the world is two-sided and profound. The mass media tend to oversimplify and thus to distort. How, then, can broadcasting function on behalf of the church?

One approach is to admit that radio and television are incapable of communicating the larger aspects of Christian truth and to search for other, less demanding functions. According to this view broadcasting has peculiar characteristics which limit its usefulness to a narrow segment of the church's task, such as public relations or "climate-creation," quite different from the functions of the pulpit, the classroom, home visitation, or even the press.

Partial Communication Without Distortion

But is the problem of the Christian broadcaster so different from the task of communicating through other media? Or is the difference one of degree rather than of kind? From its beginning the church has been unable to express the perfect wholeness of the Word. As Edwin Espy has pointed out, "It is impossible for us to communicate the full Gospel. Only Christ has manifested the Father in his fulness. Whenever we preach or teach the Word, or even when we administer the Sacraments, what we do is conditioned and partial. We communicate something of the Gospel, but we also impede it." He refers to the limitations on our religious publications, our educational programs, our dramatic presentations, our architecture, paintings and music, and even our worship services, and he concludes:

"We must recognize that in any human situation we are presenting something less than the full Gospel. What we are called to do is to witness as we are given to witness, knowing our word—even over the air waves—has feet of clay; but speaking it with integrity, making sure that it exalts to the best of our finite ability Him whom we proclaim. This is a matter of harmony, dimension, proportion, perspective, balance. The Gospel as we are able to present it is necessarily limited, but let it not be a distortion, a perversion, a truncation, and hence a violation of Christ and the church."[1]

We can search for aspects of the church's task which lend themselves most readily to accomplishment through the mass media, but in this partial communication there need not be drastic distortion. A single molecule of water contains both hydrogen and oxygen in the same proportion as in a reservoir. Each fragment of the church's communicative attempt may retain the double character of the Word, the balance or tension between nature and grace, creation and redemption, transcendence and immanence. Each program element can have the relevance of participation without capitulation.

To explore what this means in practice we shall deal with four possible purposes for Christian broadcasts: climate-creation, worship, instruction, and evangelism.

Climate-Creation: Institutional

"Climate-creation" seems out of place alongside the other three categories, but it is a concept so prevalent in religious broadcasting that it demands attention. The term itself is an unfortunate one, suggesting either unmitigated presumption or such a dubious, manipulative venture as rain making, but what is intended might also be expressed in the biblical analogy, "plowing the soil." It is a preliminary step, the preparation of listener-viewers to be receptive to the more direct ministry of the churches. Some thoughtful churchmen believe that this is the only effective function of religious broadcasting. There are such handicaps in using the entertainment-oriented media to proclaim the Word that a goal which seems more easily attainable has understandable appeal. Perhaps radio and television should not be expected to do more than encourage people to consider associating themselves with a worshiping community where conditions are much more favorable for learning the essence of the Christian faith and actually participating in the Christian life.

Both the wisdom and the weaknesses of this view become more apparent when the process of "creating a climate" is analyzed. One means of climate-creation is to convey a favorable image, in this case of the church and perhaps its clergy. This is comparable to the "institutional advertising" of industry, where no attempt is made to sell specific merchandise but the corporation is portrayed as benevolent and reliable.

In our society there are undoubtedly many persons who do not realize that the church is actively concerned with the day-to-day needs of men. Radio and television are media of immediacy, and the church, which is too often identified in the minds of men with the hazy past or improbable future, has the opportunity to proclaim its relevance to the here and now. It can and should use the mass media for responsible Christian commentary on society. The "Sunday morning look" should be dispelled along with the religious equivalent of "tired blood." Nonchurchgoers should learn that within the church there may be controversy, laughter, excitement, and enthusiastic commitment.

Various types of programs attempt to achieve this purpose. Some news programs, dealing either with "religious" news or with a Christian's interpretation of "secular" news, attempt to suggest the virility and relevance of the Christian faith. Counseling programs portray the minister as approachable and understanding. Dramatic series deal with pressing moral and ethical issues, hoping to dispose people favorably to consider association with an institution sufficiently alert to sponsor such programs. European churchmen are experimenting with revues, featuring songs, dances, and sketches, demonstrating that the Christian faith should not be divorced from any aspect of life, religious or secular.

Almost nothing is known concerning the outcome of these attempts. The few broadcasters who cite cases of individuals brought into relationship with a congregation through their programs are not often the ones experimenting with "climate-creation" and there is no research as yet providing reliable measurement.

Valid research would be extremely difficult to undertake because advocates of institutional climate-creation admit that no single broadcast is likely to have an observable result but contend that one or more broadcasts might contribute to an accumulation of impressions from many sources, the totality of which might motivate a person to consider attending worship services or affiliating with a local congregation. Even if the contribution of broadcasting to such a process proves to be measurable, there is a basic question yet to be asked: is the image of the church portrayed by each program in accord with the true nature of Christianity?

For some this will be no problem. They will argue that anything which attracts people to a congregational activity is good, no matter how unrepresentative, irrelevant, or incongruous it may be. They hold that the end justifies any means, a position long repudiated by thoughtful Protestants. They also reveal an unbiblical preoccupation with mere numbers and statistics. They identify numerical size with strength and vigor but in both biblical and post-biblical history there is usually an inverse relationship between the two.

This is not to say that congregations should deliberately avoid growing in size; it does say that numbers alone are not significant and that any portrayal of an institution which conceals or disguises its basic function is deceitful. It can be downright dangerous to attract persons to church on flimsy pretexts. A broadcast which portrays the church as "a nice organization to which to belong" will be devastating in terms of preparing for confrontation by the

Gospel. In view of broadcasting's tendency to reinforce existing attitudes it will be easy to suggest that the church fits in with existing values, that it is a sort of inexpensive country club which will provide social contacts, respectability, and a vague sort of "lift." If a person does respond to such institutional advertising, instead of being favorably disposed to consider the genuine Christian option, he is much more likely to be immunized against it by repeated inoculations of a weakened extract from the real thing.

This danger will be minimized if the image of the church is presented as accurately as possible, rather than being prettily colored. A distorted image is not inevitable. If the double character of the communication is maintained, even in the most fragmentary presentations, the distortion may be avoided. If one spot announcement promises, "Bring your troubles to church and leave them there," a following one might warn, "Bring your troubles to church—and if you pay any attention to what happens, you'll get some more . . . but you may also receive the strength to face your troubles, both the old ones and the new."

One denomination tried a similar approach with the following spot announcement:

> If you are planning to go to church this Easter because you haven't been there since last Christmas, and if you have spent some money on clothing which will be appropriate to the occasion, please stay away!
>
> I mean that! Please stay away from church this Easter if you haven't been there for months, because obviously you don't know what it's all about and the space you take will make it just that much more crowded for those who have come to worship. There are still some people, you

know, who believe that the point of Easter is the Resurrection of Christ, and that the aftermath of Easter is faithful service to the Lord. They shouldn't have to be bothered with crowds of folks who don't get the point and who don't care to serve.

If you decide to go anyway, won't you have enough courtesy towards God to dress so quietly that nobody notices you and to listen so intently that you notice no one else? It may be that for once, this Easter, you will understand, and from then on talk-like-I've-been-talking will be for someone else.[2]

To convey a faithful image of the church it is also important for religious broadcasting to portray clergymen with accuracy. Churches and commercial producers responsive to churches often attempt to make a clerical character so much of a superman that he becomes inhuman. The typical clergyman of the media appears to be so detached, aloof, and free from temptation that no one weighed down with the burdens of human existence would dream of coming to him. The mass media offer the opportunity to demonstrate that clergymen are not necessarily either pietists or "jolly good fellows," but may be authentic human beings. *The British Weekly* offered the following comment on a BBC television program MEETING POINT:

Three clerics gathered as clerics . . . and—if you will forgive the word—"discussed" Christian Unity, such as it is. . . . They were awfully nice fellows, first names and all that, and the picture of congenital anemia they presented was the standard version of Christian courtesy, charity and pointlessness as it is understood by the public on the evidence of their National Health bifocals. . . . Can nothing be done to improve BBC studio television re-

ligion? . . . The first necessary improvement is to devise
ways of presenting parsons as persons. . . . Why do we
chatter about the so-called "problem of communication"
when in the field of religious communication we must
know by now that it is largely the catching up of one
personality by another? Recently T. W. Manson took part
in a television program in which, for a few minutes, he
talked quietly on his own. He seemed to speak with the
wisdom of the ages and from long, deep, firsthand experience. Manson, Huddleston—they come over as persons
who know at firsthand whereof they speak. They look
as if life had touched them enough to roughen them
and maybe even soil them. They do not look like the over-
washed, over-groomed clerics, who, says the cruel camera,
are speaking per pro. . . . Could we have . . . then, fewer
smooth, spruce and scrubbed clerical professionals; more
of the life-worn, life-battered veterans who speak to us
out of the riches that are manifest in their very refusal to
try to persuade us about anything—who seem to be say-
ing simply: this is what I know, but I can only repeat it,
you must find it for yourself.[3]

Climate-Creation: Ideological

Another concept of climate-creation is ideological rather
than institutional. S. Franklin Mack expressed it in this
way: "Perhaps it could be argued that the function of the
media for religion is not to communicate the Gospel but
to dispose people to a consideration of those issues of life
which can be resolved only by moving toward Jesus Christ
and the church."[4]

In this sense "creating a climate" could mean to awaken
or to stimulate an awareness of a need for something or
someone beyond ourselves, an awareness of an existing in-
completeness and alienation. The 1957 World Conference

on Christian Broadcasting adopted a statement expressing the hope of broadcasters "to bring the judgment of Christ to bear upon our culture, and to speak to the condition of modern man . . . to stab awake, to disturb complacency, and to create a tension between what is and what ought to be. . . ."[5] This alienation is essentially what the biblical writers call sin. Advocates of climate-creation may be dismayed by this translation, fearing that the proclamation of man's sinfulness will obstruct rather than assist the church in its communicative task, but this prospect never discouraged the Old Testament prophets, John the Baptist, or Jesus Christ. It is even clear that the concept of sin, if not the Word, has both significance and fascination for modern man. In view of current dissatisfactions and frustrations this appears to be one point where broadcasting could exercise its power to "reinforce" on behalf of the church.

Some theologians contend that true awareness of man's situation cannot be achieved apart from the proclamation of the Word, that only in the light of the Gospel are the right questions asked and ultimate needs recognized. Dr. Mack's description of climate-creation does not indicate that a program itself must make any reference to Jesus Christ or the church, but the church would be identified with the program in a closing announcement and the church could then undertake to present the Christian option as a separate function apart from the mass media, in its more personal approaches.

This places the main burden of the communication process on the local congregation, where it undoubtedly belongs, but it also raises a question as to whether or not this is as much help as a congregation can expect from a church-sponsored broadcast. Would not a commercially-sponsored drama serve as well if carefully utilized? Without any reference to Christ or the church the exposure of human issues is a truncated contribution if Joseph Sittler is correct in maintaining, "We are not predisposed toward God any more than we are predisposed toward no God. I am predisposed both ways."[6]

There are different ways, however, of making reference to Christ and the church. Some have authenticity and integrity; others have neither. Both commercial and religious broadcasting have more than enough repetitious harangue; there is need in religious radio-television for experimentation with suggestion and subtlety rather than hammering didacticism. It should be possible for a dramatist to illuminate the human situation in such a way as to suggest that there is something meaningful in the Christian symbols.

A provocative observation by Hendrik Kraemer is applicable to this problem:

> In many cases a too immediate recourse to the fundamental theological reality behind the drama of human communication, coupled with a neglect of these secondary (psychological, cultural and sociological) factors, is a damaging simplification and a cause of complete breakdown of communications between Christian thinkers and the world. As in all things, one must be theological at the right moment, and not at every moment, which is a great art.[7]

"Climate-creation" is a fuzzy concept requiring considerable refinement before it can have meaning in religious broadcasting. If it is merely a publicity attempt to create a favorable impression on behalf of the church it may only deceive broadcasters or listener-viewers or both. We may spray many innocuous programs into the electronic atmosphere where they will disappear without making the slightest change in the fog of complacent congeniality. When we are most successful in terms of twentieth-century public relations we may fail in Christian terms.

When, however, our purpose is more substantial and authentic, when climate-creation is an aid toward people's understanding of the nature of the Word of God in its promise and its judgment, in its claims upon human beings and upon their relationships to one another in their culture, it is possible that we may help to prepare persons for the communication of the Gospel.

This is a complex task, owing partly to the nature of our message, partly to the characteristics of the media, and partly to the cultural conditions within which we work. In twentieth-century America radio and television support the prevailing theme that man is basically self-sufficient and that minor weaknesses may be remedied by products, pills, and political panaceas, that there is no need for any such drastic reorientation as demanded by Christianity. It is bound to be difficult for a few scattered programs on behalf of the church to make changes in this fundamental climate. Our only hope is in programs which remain faithful to the Word and to the nature of the church entrusted with the task of its communication. Even if such faithfulness limits the number of listener-viewers, an assumption which is not universally true, it will not reduce the ultimate effectiveness of our mission.

The attempt to create a climate (perhaps better described as the attempt to awaken or prepare a person) is a desirable function of the mass media on behalf of the church, but it is not an easy function nor is it the only one and it may not necessarily be the most productive one. Too much, therefore, must not be expected of it.

Programs of Worship

A second function of the church's ministry through the mass media is the provision for programs of worship and inspiration. From its earliest days radio has been used to transmit worship services. Factors of cost and complexity have limited the development of televised worship programs, but between the two media there is a very large number of worship and devotional broadcasts, in many cases presented by dubious representatives of the Christian community and in most cases produced with a disregard for the artistic characteristics of the media. This condition has led some religious broadcasters to reject the worship program completely and to maintain that it serves no purpose. They often rationalize this position by arguing that such programs by nature are bound to attract fewer listener-viewers than other types and that the audience attracted will include a few nonchurchgoers. There is evidence to question this assumption.

It is true that national radio or television programs using a "worship format" usually have low ratings according to conventional audience-measuring systems, but other national religious broadcasts employing different formats seldom enjoy significantly larger ratings, suggesting that more than one factor is operative. Local surveys during the past decade in such different communities as Lancaster, Pennsylvania, Waco, Texas, Madison, Wisconsin, and Los Angeles, California, indicate that it is possible for a devotional or worship program to attract a sizable audience including a substantial percentage of unchurched persons.

Such surveys are sometimes misinterpreted by persons who do not understand the media. When figures reveal that a higher percentage of regular churchgoers than of nonchurchgoers tunes to a particular program, the program is regarded as an ineffective vehicle for reaching the unchurched. This hasty conclusion overlooks the principle of self-selection whereby most of the listeners to opera already like opera and most viewers of boxing are already ring addicts. Using the mass media to attract any substantial number of people outside an interest group is an accomplishment, and it is not at all surprising that an even larger number of the "faithful" are attracted in the process. In a Los Angeles survey among 206 occasional and nonchurchgoers, 107 were found to listen either "regularly" or "some" to religious programs, which is a much better record of "outreach" than any other activity of most churches.[8]

Similar results were reported in a thorough study undertaken in Great Britain, where the Audience Research Department of the BBC analyzed the differences between listeners and nonlisteners to BBC religious radio broadcasts, almost all of which at the time (1955) could be classified in the devotional category. Though it should be recognized that the listeners under the British system did not have the option of choosing from among as many simultaneous programs as are possible in America, the findings of the British study are significant. R. J. E. Silvey, Head of the BBC Audience Research, in commenting on the results, said:

"While it is true that listening to religious broadcasts is much more common amongst churchgoers than amongst nonchurchgoers, it is certainly not true that religious broadcasts are ignored by all nonchurchgoers. We found that a quarter of them listen to religious broadcasts frequently and a further quarter occasionally. That, I suggest, is a fact of considerable significance: it means that religious broadcasting is a means whereby the influence of

Christian teaching and Christian worship is brought to bear in some degree upon half the people who are outside the churches."[9]

Such substantial possibilities cannot be ignored. The British study also revealed that one service which was more experimental and less traditional than others attracted a larger percentage of occasional and nonchurchgoers. If, instead of rejecting worship forms, there is some creativity in planning them for the broadcast media, surprising numbers of unchurched people may become listener-viewers.

There is no wisdom, either, in disregarding churchgoers as an appropriate audience for religious broadcasts. In theory most Americans are included in this category; in 1958, 63 per cent of the population regarded themselves as church members. There are important reasons why they should be taken into account in planning religious programs:

1. Only a minority of church members have a regular, continuing contact with the Christian community.
2. Many congregations conduct only one weekly worship service, and members who happen to be working at 11:00 A.M. Sundays, as millions must, will be especially in need of services broadcast at other times.
3. There are always many shut-ins, both permanent and temporary, who want and need such broadcasts.
4. Even the members who regularly attend the services of a local congregation have every reason to participate in additional broadcast services. Their experience may be enriched by exposure to other traditions, and they may be stimulated by the preaching; no single preacher can exhaust the meaning of the Christian gospel. Exposure to the great who will never be

guest preachers in their local pulpits may deepen the faith of many Christians.

5. Christians may thus be strengthened for undertaking the work of personal evangelism. As has been noted, the media are demonstrably more capable of reinforcement of attitudes and convictions than in achieving changes. Churchgoers reinforced in their convictions by broadcasts may approach unchurched acquaintances on a person-to-person basis which is likely to be more effective for this purpose than the mass media.

At the same time it must be admitted that this program type has obvious weaknesses. For some persons already reluctant to affiliate with a congregation the broadcast services may become a substitute for a more direct relationship. Even if the broadcaster makes a conscious effort to encourage alignment with a local fellowship of Christians, it is difficult for listener-viewers to become participants rather than mere spectators. The choir and organ may be superior to the music in a neighborhood congregation, but a person is unlikely to join in the singing while sitting at home. The whole listening-viewing situation is different from one where believers have congregated for corporate worship. It is true that worshipers in the church may be disturbed by restless children, coughing neighbors, or low-flying aircraft but there are usually greater distractions in the home. In the early days of televising services cameramen were encouraged to seek out novel "reaction" or "human interest" shots, thus providing a completely disruptive influence for the viewer interested in worshiping. More recently, however, most such telecasts are produced with better taste.

The preaching in broadcast services presents its own problems. There are many devoted, respected pastors who have much of value to say to members that know and love them, but who have great difficulty in holding the attention of unknown, noncaptive audiences. Care must be exercised in selecting ministers to represent the church on radio and television. This selectivity, however, must not go to extremes. The broadcasting industry is convinced of the appeal of familiar personalities, and the search for capable oral communicators may lead to the creation of what Malcolm Boyd terms "celebrity-gods," clerical pin-up boys whose ministry becomes warped by the pressures of publicity. A commission of the British Council of Churches issued a thoughtful statement concerning this problem:

It is not the present policy of the Corporation (BBC) to allow its programmes to be used to "build up" national reputations except for those who can be classed as entertainers. The Commission believes this to be right in religious broadcasting. No one person can speak adequately for the whole church, and the spiritual strain and the many temptations that would beset such a "religious personality" are in themselves sufficient to make such a course unwise. But something could be done to reap some of the benefits of the intimacy that frequent and regular broadcasting establishes. . . . A pool of experienced and successful broadcasters might be given a good percentage of broadcasting time each year; listeners might thus find the satisfactions and benefits of hearing the well-known voice without the broadcasters being subjected to undesirable strains.[10]

Probably the most certain conclusion concerning worship broadcasts is that not everyone who sees or hears a worship program will engage in worship. At worst it may be another "show"; more positively, it may at least be a source of information, overlapping our next category of program purposes, which follows the category of programs of worship.

Instructional Programs

A third possible program function for the media on behalf of the church is that of instruction. It should be possible for radio and television programs to explain the Christian faith and to portray experiences and relationships of the Christian life and work in home, church, community, and world. Since the media are known to affect ideas and opinions which are new both to the individual and his group, the church could help a community to face current issues by broadcasting relevant information quickly before positions were solidified.

Here, again, the prospective audience is not limited to churchgoers. Programs such as a children's television series correlated with church school curricula can supplement, enrich, and perhaps correct the educational efforts of local congregations, but this does not mean that non-churchgoers will be uninterested. Whether or not there is a genuine "return to religion" in contemporary America there is undoubtedly curiosity about religion. Questioning teen-agers, existentialist college students, and adult readers of popular magazines demonstrate in different ways an interest in religion. Stanley Hopper has expressed the opinion that when a solidly theological statement is made, "There is a sense in which the people outside the Christian community are more amenable to the message . . . than those inside who reduce the Christian message to clichés."[11] The historic realism of Christianity may hold the attention of a generation torn between discredited optimism and despair.

The BBC Research Study already quoted searched for reasons why people listen to religious broadcasts. They found that among persons over sixty-five years of age the most commonly endorsed phrase was, "I find them comforting." Among those fifty to sixty-five years of age another reason was a close second, "They help me to cope with daily life." Those between thirty and fifty gave almost equal weight to these two reasons and to a third: that religious broadcasts "helped them to understand what Christianity means." Among the under-thirties it was this desire for help in understanding Christianity which was, by an ample margin, most commonly endorsed.[12] Yet many religious broadcasters hoping to include younger people in their audiences disregard this desire for understanding; instead of offering instruction for which they are uniquely qualified they try lamely to imitate variety shows which others are more capable of producing.

Not many audiences for instructional broadcasts will be vast, in mass media terms, although an occasional program will be surprisingly appealing: one radio series in Wingham, Ontario, featuring news and comment from a Christian perspective enjoyed the highest rating of any daytime program on the station. But even when this is not the case the church is accustomed to working through minorities and by means of the mass media may be in touch with a much larger minority than would ordinarily be the case. Dr. Huston Smith of Washington University says: "The course which I taught over educational television was the most exhilarating experience of my life. Within six weeks of the morning 'The Religions of Man' was conceived, I was teaching to an estimated weekly audience of 100,000

—approximately ten times the number of students I could otherwise have expected to teach during a fifty-year career."[13]

In Washington, D. C., a weekly average of 85,000 people, including physicians, lawyers, professors, and military officials, watched an hour-long biblical television program on the life of Jesus. The series had the highest audience rating of four programs telecast simultaneously in the area. Viewers were encouraged to be more than mere spectators. Two thousand persons secured a syllabus and registered for the course; two hundred of them enrolled on a credit basis making it possible to submit assignments and take examinations. Field trips, attracting hundreds of persons, were made to the Washington Cathedral and the National Gallery of Art.[14]

Even when instructional broadcasts do not transmit great quantities of information they may stimulate interest which will lead to private investigation and reflection. This is the principal function of discussion programs which often appear to confuse issues rather than clarify them.

The familiar limitations of the media must be kept in mind in planning instructional programs. For example, the absence of a direct person-to-person relationship handicaps any attempt to engage in counseling over the air. In many parts of the country there are radio and television programs offering to answer questions submitted by listener-viewers. Some are scheduled late at night when sustaining broadcast time is readily available and when sleepless, disturbed persons may happen to be tuned in. Such programs offer to some people the same surreptitious invasion of privacy made possible by party-line telephones. In avoiding this trap the broadcaster can make it clear that some questions cannot be considered soberly without knowing a great deal more about the questioner. He can also make it clear, if he will, that in any case he does not possess the answers to all questions. Failure to exercise such caution can be disastrous. On the other hand, a carefully planned question-and-answer program can demonstrate the depth and breadth of a Christian's concern and resources.

Possibilities for Evangelism

A fourth functional area of the church's ministry is evangelism, embracing not only verbal proclamation of the good news but encounter, engagement, and enlistment. Evangelism attempts to break down or reach across the barriers between the church and persons outside, whether they are antagonistic, lukewarm, or lapsed. As applied to the mass media almost everyone will regard this as a doubtful category for good but different reasons. Some will argue that it is impossible to accomplish evangelism in the sense of conversion through such impersonal media; others will contend that there should be no separate category for evangelism because all the other categories—climate-creation, worship, and instruction—involve elements of evangelism.

These two positions are not diametrically opposite but represent two aspects of one idea: seldom, if ever, does a single broadcast bring about a fundamental reorientation in a person's religious convictions, but many different types of programs, whether or not their primary objective is evangelism, may contribute toward the process.

There is resistance to radio and television evangelism from two principal sources, one within industry and the other within the church. Although commercial broadcasting thrives on propaganda for specific products the industry is wary of programs which become very specific in terms of religious commitment, partly because there have been unscrupulous "quacks" in religious broadcasting and management is understandably hesitant to become an arbiter of theological doctrine. Many program executives, however, realize that this is not sufficient reason to deny responsible broadcasters the right to air their deepest convictions.

Thoughtful Christians hesitate to employ broadcasting for evangelism in the fear that they may be as guilty as some commercial broadcasters of manipulation and exploitation, that they may be tempted to use "hooks" and "gimmicks" and motivation research to deceive listener-viewers. Beyond this, they have the same reservations with radio-TV evangelism that they have with other forms of mass evangelism. Parker, Barry, and Smythe listed common pitfalls: "the temptation to use spectacular methods; the tendency of the least stable members of an audience to be most responsive; the advocacy of simple techniques as a substitute for the long and sometimes arduous struggle for basic changes in life style; the reduction of the infinite variety of the Christian life to a stereotypical least common denominator; and the failure to attach individuals in an audience to a permanent group relationship or a permanent pastoral relationship that can build a quick emotional response into constructive and lasting character change."[15]

A careful analysis of these pitfalls will reveal that they are not confined to mass methods but exist, perhaps in lesser degree, in the use of printed media, in preaching, and even in personal visitation techniques. It also appears that the pitfalls, though serious, are not unavoidable. Faithfulness to the Word in planning broadcasts would be helpful, as would relation of the programs to the life and work of a local congregation. The question, then, must be raised as to whether there is sufficient need for the use of radio and TV in evangelism to warrant a struggle to avoid the pitfalls.

Alan Walker, among others, has commented on the crucial need to carry on the work of evangelism outside church buildings. He has observed that whenever evangelism meetings in Australia have been held in public halls or theaters or auditoriums, audiences have been two or three times larger than if meetings had been planned in church buildings. In answer to the question why people should be ready to come to public halls for such meetings but shrink from entering churches he says:

> The chief reason is that most people dislike above all else to be called hypocrites. They have the mistaken idea that to be seen entering a church building is to be making a certain Christian profession. As yet they are not willing to declare themselves Christian. . . . Also to enter a church is to be plunged into the style of worship that goes on in that church and there is fear of personal embarrassment through ignorance of procedures. . . . Perhaps the same discovery caused John Wesley to go out of the churches in his day to where the people were. Perhaps then, too, if men were to be won to the church, they had first to be met and reasoned with outside the church.[16]

Broadcasting is obviously one means for making some contact, no matter how limited, with numbers of persons who are not willing to venture into a church building. Surveys indicate that every national religious broadcast attracts to its audience many more nonchurchgoers than attend the most popular evangelistic meetings. The New

Haven Communications Research Project concluded that
three out of five households watch or listen to some religious program with regularity and that this three-fifths "is
not importantly different from the two-fifths who do not
listen." The Project reported that specific programs often
attract specialized groups, but a diversified audience is at
least a possibility.[17] (It would be completely erroneous,
however, to jump to the conclusion that any broadcast at
any time will be likely to attract a substantial percentage
of nonchurchgoers. For example, early on a Sunday morning, when many religious broadcasts are scheduled, audiences are predominantly churchgoers.)

Whether anything significant happens to listener-
viewers is another question. So long as their participation
is only passive and they have no contact with a community of believers there can be little hope for change of
attitude or decisive action. Harman Grisewood has a fresh
way of stating the problem:

> The temptation for the listener which I do not think can
> always be resisted is to acquire the habit of regarding the
> serious material that is broadcast as merely entertainment
> on a different plane; to regard the sequence of speakers—
> scientists, poets, philosophers, politicians, priests and
> scholars—as a cavalcade of "entertainers," as so many
> "acts," you might say, in an intellectual cabaret, with-
> out realizing that what is said is either true or not true
> and that ultimately some decision must be reached.[18]

An evangelism mission in Scotland attempted to overcome this handicap in the use of the media and concluded
that significant results could be expected from religious
broadcasts only when local congregations set up listening
groups and carried on follow-up activities. The same
broadcast which went without notice in one community

144

where the local congregations paid no attention to it produced measurable results with nonchurchgoers in another community where a congregation integrated the broadcast into over-all evangelism efforts.[19] Several American denominations have had similar experiences with nationally distributed television series. There is abundant evidence that the element of local participation, discussion, study, and action in relation to broadcasts may be one of the greatest means available for strengthening the impact of radio and television religious programs.

Need for Planned Diversity

Our survey of possible employment of the mass media in major functional areas of the church's task has revealed no single area where the media can be enlisted without difficulty. On the other hand, neither is there an area where the media are useless. There is undoubtedly much overlapping among program functions. A broadcast intended to evangelize unchurched people may serve primarily as a worship experience for the faithful; a program prepared as a devotional service may instead serve an informational purpose; an instructional broadcast may create climate in the sense of awakening persons; any program may contribute in greater or lesser degree to evangelism. To some extent this overlapping is due to lack of clear objectives on the part of broadcasters, but it will never be eliminated because of the varying backgrounds and conditions of listener-viewers.

The search for a single, winning format to attract all churchgoers has no sound basis. The BBC Study previously cited found that nonchurchgoers "show no signs of welcoming religious plays more than religious talks or discussions." Approximately the same percentage of nonchurchgoers indicated an interest in religious talks and discussions as in plays about religious subjects. Among occasional churchgoers there was only slightly more interest in discussions and plays than in talks.[20] Of course nonchurchgoers might be attracted by plays not identified as religious but this does not upset the general finding that nonchurchgoers may be attracted in considerable numbers by different types of programs.

Instead of a formula for a "successful series" the church needs a planned diversity of programs, faithfully serving different functions in different ways. The matter of format appears to be less significant than factors such as artistic quality, theological integrity, contagious persuasiveness of personal conviction, and local follow-up.

A denomination or council of churches may produce series as different in form as straight talk, interview, and drama, but reach virtually the same audience with all three because the themes, language, and approach are so similar. On the other hand, a series of interviews (or talks or dramas) may be so varied in style and language that different audiences are attracted at different times.

Some program forms, of course, have greater flexibility than others, but any format may reach a sizable audience; no format will attract everyone. Variety is desirable, not just for the sake of variety, but for the sake of listener-viewers who are in various conditions of mind and stages of religious readiness.

Some persons, including both churchgoers and non-churchgoers, are sufficiently concerned with questions of life's meaning that they will give attention to programs which deal directly with vital issues; in fact they are likely to be impatient with indirection. Others will tune out any program which appears to demand much from them in terms of response. The same person may be in different frames of mind at different times. There is room for experimentation with varied approaches, avoiding imitation, on the one hand, of programs devised for use in the setting of church buildings and imitation, on the other hand, of programs devised for secular-commercial interests.

The New Haven Communications Research Project pointed out the importance of a programing policy based upon "a well-developed theory about society, community and personality in our time," a policy which would "see the potential audience in all the complexity of human dynamics in our anxiety-driven, class-conditioned, striving and mobile age." Such a policy would identify groups to whom religion intends to speak and work toward the development of programs prepared specifically for them. Warning against the danger of a program so "successful" by the standards of the industry that the fundamental purposes of the Christian church would be ignored or denied, the major report of the Project commented, "In this field as in any other there is no spectacular substitute for the responsible ministry which sees each individual human being as a child of God and speaks to each heart on terms that are relevant to its condition."

The authors of the report regarded this as its central and most important finding: "that in programing for religious use of the mass media, the ingenuity and flexibility of the planners must match the complexity of needs and circumstances of the potential audience. It must reflect the diversity of ministry of the churches themselves, and if indeed these media are to emphasize communication to the outsider—which is the claim most often made for them —then their form must be as free, imaginative and uninhibited by conventional church pattern as it is possible to be while remaining within the framework of purpose set by the churches themselves."[21]

There is a place in religious broadcasting for different purposes—the preparation or awakening which broadcasters call climate-creation, worship, instruction, and evangelism, among others; for different types of programs —talk, discussion, music, drama, news, interview, documentary, variety, and some yet to be developed; and for different audiences—children, teen-agers, young parents, the retired, searching intellectuals, frustrated factory workers, and all other segments of society. Achieving such purposeful, creative diversity and utilizing its values require action by individuals, local congregations, denominations, and councils of churches.

CHAPTER 7

In Pursuit of a Plan

The church in the world of radio-television has work to do. It would be convenient if a committee would formulate a comprehensive but specific plan which could then be executed by a staff of specialists, but such a master plan is not now in existence and may never be feasible. The church's opportunities and possibilities in relation to the mass media are so complex that there must be years of experimentation and exploration before much is known about them. What emerges eventually will certainly be less of a blueprint than a flexible strategy, subject always to revisions in the light of changing conditions.

Co-ordination of Effort

In pursuit of a plan there should be explorations into many fields: art, theology, sociology, and communications research, among others. For such ventures to have the most meaning and contribute to long-range planning there is need for more co-ordination of effort among Protestant and Orthodox churches.

The nature of the American system of broadcasting would seem to make some form of co-operation among religious groups inescapable. Both nationally and locally there is a limit to the amount of time generally available for religious broadcasting. In a pluralistic society this must be allocated fairly among Protestants, Catholics, and Jews, plus others if they are sufficiently represented in a particular area.

In dealing with government, with stations and networks, and with each other, all groups have common problems unrelated to the differences in their theological positions. They share the desire to make a prophetic witness in a materialistic culture. They may differ in what they have to say, but their best hope of maintaining the freedom to say it lies in defending the rights of all. Far from compromising distinctive beliefs this form of co-ordination protects their chance to be expressed. In the absence of co-operation among religious groups a station or network may stifle variety either by selecting one or two viewpoints as broadly representative of the lot or by stipulating that all religious broadcasts must be so innocuously neutral that they lose all flavor.

The three major faiths have achieved a significant measure of co-ordination in working with NBC and CBS in the production of various series. The Protestant and Orthodox communions belonging to the National Council have their own co-operative agency, the Broadcasting and Film Commission. Many clergymen whose churches do not belong to the National Council are affiliated with the National Association of Religious Broadcasters.

Representatives of denominations both within and outside the National Council have been participating, since 1958, in a series of Consultations on Protestant Religious Broadcasting. In these meetings Protestant radio and television broadcasters have discussed common problems and opportunities in an effort to improve standards and to increase the effectiveness of programs. Participants united "in commending radio and TV stations and networks which, by their handling of public service programing, show that they aim to serve the best interests of the community or communities in which they are to be heard." They also expressed the belief that "radio and television stations and networks should include high-quality religious programs, whether on a paid or a sustaining basis, at times mutually acceptable to the religious broadcasters and to the radio and television stations and networks." In an effort to improve relations between religious broadcasters and the industry they adopted what is described as a code of standards for the evaluation of religious broadcasts.[1]

It includes one provision dealing with reputable sponsorship, another guarding against abuses in financial support and accountability, a third advocating program promotion, and a fourth admonishing religious broadcasters to be courteous and ethical in their conduct. The only section actually dealing with program evaluation is couched in very general terms ("Religious programs should be presented reverently and constructively . . . and should conform to the highest broadcasting standards."), and there is no provision, of course, for its implementation.

This particular effort at co-ordination is worthwhile and commendable, so far as it goes. At least it recognizes that Protestants who differ in many respects have common problems in dealing with the mass media in a democracy. Beyond the conditions imposed by a pluralistic society, however, there are other reasons for Protestant co-ordination. If the need for a planned diversity of programs is to be taken seriously there must be a structured strategy involving as many Protestant broadcasters as possible in the co-ordination of program planning, production, promotion, utilization, and research. The expenses of broadcasting, especially in television, are so great that some form of cost sharing among congenial groups would seem to be obligatory as an elementary form of financial stewardship.

For so comprehensive an effort it may be too much to expect so broad a denominational representation as achieved in the Consultations on Protestant Religious Broadcasting. A Christian cannot dismiss the thought of what a more united witness would mean to our society nor can he put aside the memory of Christ's prayer "that they all may be one," but the problems of divided Protestantism are bound to be reflected in any co-operative venture. In Protestantism a single, central administration may be undesirable and is apparently impossible. The alternative, however, need not be chaotic duplication and waste.

Locally and regionally there are many attempts to co-ordinate Protestant broadcasting through ministerial associations and councils of churches. In many cases this is merely a matter of allocating available sustaining time on stations in the area among the community's clergymen. In scattered places, however, steps are being taken to provide balanced schedules of religious broadcasts.

Nationally the Broadcasting and Film Commission has been working toward a planned diversity of programs on behalf of the National Council of Churches. For children the filmed series, OFF TO ADVENTURE, is distributed to television stations. LOOK UP AND LIVE, on CBS-TV, is a creative and experimental attempt to make contact with youth. Among the programs prepared for adults NATIONAL RADIO PULPIT on NBC-radio is a program of preaching and worship, ART OF LIVING, also on NBC-radio, attempts to express in colloquial terms the relationship of Christianity to daily living, and PILGRIMAGE on ABC-radio also serves an instructional function through provocative discussion of issues and events. FRONTIERS OF FAITH on NBC-TV is directed to searching minds in an effort at climate-creation.

Despite national, regional, and local efforts to achieve purposeful diversity, thoughtful observers of American religious broadcasting cannot be very optimistic when they note the following conditions:

1. National religious programs offered by the networks are refused by many affiliates who would probably carry them if there were active encouragement from local churches.

2. National and local programs often go on the air without promotion from local congregations.

3. Both a partial cause and a partial result of the two conditions above is the current network practice of scheduling their two major religious TV programs, LOOK UP AND LIVE and FRONTIERS OF FAITH, at hours when churchgoers can seldom view them. Time is also divided on both series among the three faiths, a condition which no commercial sponsor would tol-

erate for a season. The argument that these programs are directed to the unchurched does not justify their placement when it is recalled that for any
effective utilization of such broadcasts there should
be follow-up dialogue with Christian acquaintances
who have also seen the programs.

4. In many communities there is an abundance of a
single type of broadcast for one segment of the audience while other types and groups are neglected.

5. BFC producers are fully aware of the shortcomings
of current National Council programs. They are
handicapped by a serious lack of resources, a condition which could grow worse if constituent denominations, instead of strengthening existing programs,
should continue to undertake new productions which
often duplicate rather than supplement current efforts.

Along with local and regional approaches to the problems above there must be a re-examination of the function of a Protestant broadcasting agency such as the present Broadcasting and Film Commission. In the early days
of the BFC few National Council denominations had
radio-TV staffs, and it was taken for granted that the BFC
would produce all programs on their behalf. With the
appointment of denominational staffs and the allocation of
denominational budgets there is a growing conviction that
this procedure is undesirable, or at least unrealistic.

In recent years there has been an increase in the number
of programs financed by individual denominations, including members of the National Council. Several bodies are
spending much larger sums on single series of their own
than is being contributed by all the Council members to-

ward the co-operative efforts of the Broadcasting and Film Commission. This is partly a concession to expediency; despite all the talk about church unity it is still easier to raise a million dollars for a denominational than for an interdenominational project and denominational radio-TV staffs are humanly eager for recognition of their new departments. To some extent, however, the trend results from considered opinions that it is wiser to place responsibility in a single denominational staff or committee than in a more cumbersome commission responsible to many different denominations. Denominations also have the most direct lines of communication with local churches, so important for promotion and utilization. In addition, Protestants are traditionally wary of anything suggesting a "superchurch."

If this view becomes the basis for reorientation, the BFC or a successor will not concentrate on the joint production of programs, but will co-ordinate the individual efforts of constituent denominations. There will be consultation among all interested parties before national series are developed or aired, followed by co-operative promotion and utilization, but production responsibilities will often be placed in denominational hands. Every attempt will be made to integrate the ideas, research, productions, and total resources of all denominations into a structured strategy, but the BFC will not attempt to be a collective programing entity.

The alternative to this "service agency" concept is that of a "delegated representative," according to which the Broadcasting and Film Commission or a similar agency would be authorized to undertake all broadcasting for member communions. This would require a delegation of responsibility presently opposed by certain denominations, along with the allocation of a Commission budget many times its present size.

There may be an acceptable point some distance from either of these two extremes, but the prevailing concept must be determined and the function of the BFC more clearly defined by its participating denominations. Until then the BFC staff is in an impossible position. This decision is one which should be made at the highest levels of policy making. Top officials of the denominations must be called upon to grapple with the problem.

Whatever the form of co-ordination eventually decided upon, there will be no restrictions on distinctive theological expressions. Representatives of member communions are presently free to articulate their beliefs on National Council programs. Edwin Espy has made it clear that "the desire of the ecumenical movement for the expression of the church's unity is not posited on the suppression of the church's diversity. On the contrary the very concept of the wholeness of the Gospel is based on the premise that the Gospel is richer than any single manifestation of it, and that every honest manifestation is to be honored as a part of the whole."[2]

This means, of course, that some broadcasts are bound to be less than satisfactory to all Protestants. The Board of Managers of the Broadcasting and Film Commission has stated: "Because National Council broadcasts reflect a wide range of point of view, it is inevitable that some segments of programing will not be fully acceptable to all constituents. Therefore, if parts of National Council programing are at times inconsistent with one another, this should be viewed in light of the fact that there are varied and even opposing points of view within the Council constituency."[3]

As noted earlier, it is to be expected that each expression will be incomplete in itself. This is no reason why any presentation must be a grave distortion of the Gospel, but there will always be some disagreement as to the distinction between a partial presentation and a perversion of the Word.

Local and regional patterns for co-ordinating Protestant broadcasting are as diversified as would be expected. In some areas there is little or no co-operation, in others it extends to the three major faiths. Some councils of churches employ radio-TV executives who may broadcast on behalf of constituents, or may co-ordinate their efforts, or may do both. It is in the local community that co-ordination breaks down or becomes effective. Many of the better religious broadcasts originate locally, and the best of national programs are wasted unless they are included in the schedules of local stations and woven into the life of local congregations.

Relationship Between
Christianity and the Arts

While organizational problems are being resolved there must be continued exploration of creative ways in which the Gospel may be communicated by means of radio and television. Clergymen, familiar only with the traditions of pulpit and press, seldom think beyond strictly verbal forms of expression, but they can learn little of value from the examples of peddling pitchmen and syrupy serials. To see the possibilities in broadcasting, a person must stretch the media in his mind. Through the flexibility of radio and television all the wondrously varied faculties of the human imagination may be called upon to express the Christian faith concerning God and man. In earlier centuries and in other parts of the world Christians have expressed their deepest convictions in music, painting, poetry, sculpture, dance, and drama. Old and new creations in all these fields may be broadcast on radio or television, sometimes in exciting combinations.

Too often, however, the church's venture in religious broadcasting is made a specialized hobby and kept isolated from drama, from worship and the arts, and even from audio-visual education. When there is a crossing of lines the broadcaster may look upon art merely as a tool or technique to be used for his purposes, instead of an independent approach to truth which has its own standards and its own disciplines. He may even be impatient with art because of a characteristic it shares with revelation— the possibility of evoking responses beyond the mere transfer of concepts, often beyond the intentions or even comprehension of the human creator.

The artist, on the other hand, often does not have an appreciation for the problems of broadcasting, and his disdainful attitude may contribute to the conclusion that there is no connection between the arts and the mass media.

In taking issue with this view Amos Wilder has said:

Concern with the fine arts leads the Christian inevitably to a concern with the mass culture of the time and its symbols, since the criteria are finally the same. . . . What is important is integrity, reality, wholeness of vision. That which we call "bad art" at any level is not realism but shallowness; not sentiment but sentimentality; not imaginative escape but escapism which obscures the givens of life; not the portrayal of violence but sensational violence that lacks its context of cause and consequence. In bad art the conflicts of life are too easily resolved. We must reject all fables and fictions whether in art, or in social ideology, or in religion, which blind the reader or public to the necessities and responsibilities of our human condition.[4]

Despite the clarity of Mr. Wilder's statement it is seldom possible for churchmen to reach substantial agreement as to what is "good art" and "bad art." The years of church history in which there was a suspicion and even a rejection of art have left us with a poverty of critical and creative abilities. The appearance of almost every work of art on a religious theme is the occasion for the most extreme disagreement, as demonstrated in the controversies aroused by De Mille's "The Ten Commandments," McLeish's "J. B.," the plays of Tennessee Williams, and the motion picture, "He Who Must Die."

This is not to suggest that unanimity in these matters is either possible or desirable, but at present there is little common ground for discussion and even less genuine communication among discussants, creating a discouraging problem for the broadcasters.

Some years ago the Broadcasting and Film Commission produced a radio series which brought into focus certain issues concerning music and religion. The programs featured a brass ensemble and a vocal choir presenting "popularized arrangements" of hymns, along with a narrator. Titled, THY KINGDOM COME, the series drew many letters of praise, such as the following:

"Congratulations and commendations to the people who have been involved in preparing this program. It certainly was not one of the worn-out, stereotyped religious broadcasts which have repelled not only the unchurched but the faithful as well. It had the feel of a new venture and the thrill of an old faith expressed in new terms."

". . . I wanted to thank you, not only for the beauty of the singing and the reading of the psalms, but for the spiritual quality also, and for the good it did me."

". . . I am a college student. . . . Your program strengthened my faith in the church."

"I stumbled onto the program and listened enthralled, and when it was finished said to my husband, 'That is the kind of music you will listen to in Heaven.' . . . A wonderful preparation for the Lord's Day."

Some listeners, especially professors and ministers of music, responded differently:

". . . What I heard was my church paying to mix the Word of God with the sentimental scum and slime of modern life. In one moment I was washed clean by the Bible. The next I was smeared with offal. . . . This, I tell you, is a scandal that really ascends into heaven. . . ."

"How can a body of intelligent, cultured people really want to interlard the gospel of Jesus Christ with these cute sounds from the cocktail lounge and the Kostelanetz show? Will the next step be a telecast of the Last Supper, with perhaps a floor show by the Rockettes? There is here, in all seriousness, a very dangerous fallacy: someone thinks that music to be simple has to be poor in quality, that the good things in art are too good for the common people, that they must be offered a substitute."

The one certain result of the series was that it stimulated a healthy examination of issues and suggested the importance of a genuine exchange of ideas prior to the undertaking of any comparable experiment in the future.

More recent programs on LOOK UP AND LIVE and FRONTIERS OF FAITH have been similarly provocative. In attempting to reach out to the culturally disaffected the producers

160

sometimes find themselves in a no-man's land between Christianity and art, thus exposing the pressing need for a blending of genuine artistic creativity with theological and social sensitivity. Religion has much to learn from art, and art is not necessarily compromised by exposure to religion. Amos Wilder has said:

> It is true that Christian belief, like Marxist theory, will weaken a work of art rather than strengthen it if it be so employed as to do violence to the total work of the imagination. But all significant literary work, especially in its more ambitious forms, benefits from underlying presuppositions of order, and the Christian faith if not used in imperialist fashion is a great asset to the artist.[5]

The relation between religion and art must not be artificial and imposed upon one or the other. The blandness of many programs is due to their concoction as sugarcoated pills when they should instead be seasoned food.

It is a mistake to build a program by authorizing a committee to formulate the religious message and then hiring a clever craftsman to deliver the capsule with which to deceive an audience into swallowing the distasteful medicine. The artistic form taken by a program is an integral part of its communicative nature. Christian educators are beginning to realize this in connection with artwork used in church schools, and broadcasters must become similarly aware of the artistic dimension of programs. A theological concept may be distorted by an art form in which it is expressed, and an art form may be destroyed by a theological idea superimposed upon it, but a program may also have both artistic integrity and theological validity; this is the ideal which is enticing to contemplate but agonizing to pursue.

Continuing Research

In the development of a diversity of programs on behalf of the church there is also need for continuing research. The New Haven Communications Research Project was a significant venture, but it was intended to be only a beginning and there have been insufficient resources for additional steps.

Comparatively little is known about audience response to specific programs. Production budgets seldom include provision for research, and it is not unusual for a series to be broadcast year after year without really reliable information about its audience and its influence having been secured.

It is also desirable to learn more about the differing functions of radio and television. Now that television has become the dominant entertainment medium it would seem that listeners would be very selective in tuning to radio and that radio audiences would be much more specialized than in TV. Preliminary studies raise doubts about this; many people listen to radio when temporarily satiated with television or when a TV set is not available, as in a car or on a beach. There is also a feeling that radio has greater possibilities than TV for stimulating the imagination, for dealing with concepts in contrast with images, and for encouraging a mood conducive to quiet reflection. Yet under certain conditions the imagination, conceptual thought and reflection may be stimulated by visual as well as auditory stimuli. Additional research is necessary before there can be any valid reappraisal of the best uses for radio.

A broader area of research would reappraise the churches' operations relating their physical resources to the mass media. Do we need larger and larger buildings with more and more rooms? Is it good stewardship to invest great sums in facilities to be used for only a few hours weekly? Can radio and television be used to allow groups of people to engage in common enterprises without always assembling in a single building? To date there has been little speculation about such problems and no serious study of them.

We know little about how the American public perceives the Christian religion and the institutions of Christianity. Even within the churches it is difficult to assess attitudes as distinguished from practices and appearances. To what extent do broadcasts affect the emotion, thought, and behavior of noncaptive and invisible audiences? There are many "varieties of religious experience," and certain aspects of the experience may be unmeasurable and unpredictable; but this does not excuse us from the responsibility of knowing all that we can about the persons with whom we wish to engage in communication.

In this search we need not turn only to behavioral scientists from psychology and sociology; we can learn also from philosophers, educators, theologians, and artists. Too much weight is often given to research based upon such narrow presuppositions that it is misleading rather than revealing.

If the findings of research and the insights of art are to contribute to the purposeful diversity of religious programs they must be brought to the attention of both national and local broadcasters through workshops, seminars, conferences, and academic courses. Responsibility for this task is shared by denominations, local churches, national and regional councils, universities, colleges, and theological seminaries.

Christians not only have much to learn from research but have contributions to make to it. The church shares with industry and education the responsibility for studying the influence of the mass media on our society. Both individually and corporately we have every reason to take all possible steps to speed such basic research.

Utilization of Programs

The creation and distribution of programs, no matter how diversified and authentic, is only the beginning of the church's task in religious broadcasting. What happens locally before, during, and after the broadcasts is at least as important, but frequently disregarded. As with research, this process of "utilization" is often overlooked in program budgets.

We have noted that the same program which is virtually unnoticed in one community may have considerable influence in another. In one case the local church disregards the broadcast, in the other it is carefully correlated with regular congregational activities.

The first obvious step in utilization of broadcasts is promotion. If the churches actively used their multiple channels of publicity to inform the sixty million American Protestants about national programs and encouraged members to pass along the information to acquaintances, they could soon build audiences many times their present size. This, in turn, might encourage stations and networks to grant more desirable time for the programs. There is no reason why such promotional efforts should be reserved for broadcasts produced by the churches themselves. The program, "Monganga," on the commercial television series, THE MARCH OF MEDICINE, was an authentic portrayal of the work of a medical missionary and deserved even more than the modest promotional assistance which it received from churches.

It is not enough, however, simply to announce or publish the time and station of a broadcast. Preparation should be made for a suggested follow-up activity. On some programs, including the BFC radio series, NATIONAL RADIO PULPIT, ART OF LIVING, and PILGRIMAGE, listeners are invited to write in and request printed material, which may be a copy of the broadcast script, a bibliography, or supplemental reading. This at least encourages the listener to review and reflect on the ideas developed on the broadcast. Unfortunately, the expense of this undertaking often discourages producers from attempting it. When OFF TO ADVENTURE first went on the air so many children responded to an invitation to write in for printed material that the offer had to be modified because of budgetary limitations. There is something ironic about a situation in which some groups within the church are striving rather desperately to get people to accept free literature while another church group does not have sufficient financial resources to fulfill requests of persons asking for material.

A basic aspect of utilization is the provision for more than haphazard listening-viewing. Individual programs should be auditioned in church gatherings and discussions held concerning the meaning of the broadcast and possible integration of the series in activities of the congregation.

When a program is thus examined by an able and representative group a critical report on their behalf to the producers will help to strengthen the series. Members can also arrange to hear or view other programs in the company of unchurched friends. Discussion of the issues raised by the programs may encourage these friends to turn to the church for further enlightenment. Without some such procedure most radio and television series will mean little or nothing to a local congregation.

The most ambitious attempt in this direction is related to the TV series TALK BACK, developed by the Television, Radio, and Film Commission of the Methodist Church, produced and distributed in co-operation with the BFC. Featuring filmed dramatic incidents, the programs demonstrate the inconsistency between people's actions and their professed standards, confronting the audience with provocative questions concerning the Christian way of life. Instead of either forcing pat answers into a pseudo-dramatic mold or simply leaving the questions hanging in the airwaves, the producers plan for the following local involvement:

1. A local panel goes on the air following the film and engages in a brief discussion of the issues raised.
2. Churches are to promote the series and arrange for groups to meet at the time of the broadcast, continuing their own discussion at the end of the program.
3. Other live local postbroadcast "talk back" forums are scheduled for "neutral grounds," such as the TV studio or a community center where persons not connected with a church might be less reluctant to venture.
4. Individual viewers are offered give-aways assisting them to have their own "talk back" experiences with friends and acquaintances. The literature suggests that there are many other thought-provoking broadcasts which warrant similar discussion.
5. To plan for local production, promotion, and utilization, two-day workshops are held in each new community three months before the series is to go on the air.

Criticism of such a plan as too complex and demanding

probably reflects a basic misunderstanding of the possibilities and limitations of religious broadcasting. It is not enough to put a good program on the air. The church must also anticipate what might happen after the broadcast and cultivate it. This does not mean that every series requires a utilization plan so specifically structured as the one for TALK BACK, but there should be some provision for meaningful and demanding activities after most broadcasts.

Undertaking this follow-up task involves more than the obvious hazards of organization. If the broadcasts are truly significant and listener-viewers take them seriously they may drive a congregation to self-examination. If a nonchurchgoer is encouraged by a vital, relevant broadcast to consider involvement in the life and work of a Christian congregation he may be disillusioned by the conditions he finds. If a program for children excites interest in religious education the local church school may be disappointing.

In England the Sheffield Industrial Mission has been trying to re-establish contact between the church and the workingman through various tradition-breaking means, but after fifteen years no attempt is yet made to relate the workers to the churches of Sheffield. Canon Wickham has evidence that when a worker does venture back to one of the traditional parishes, he is all too likely to be absorbed in the institutional activities, develop a somewhat pharasaical attitude and become of little use in witnessing to the Gospel in his factory role.[6] Daniel Jenkins speaks from the background of a ministry on two continents: "Perhaps the chief obstacle in the way of effective communication today is the fact that the pattern of life of the whole Christian community does not embody clearly the nature of the gospel it professes."[7]

But has the situation ever been much different? The same statement could be made about the church of every century, including the first. While this is no excuse, neither is it cause for despair. Awareness of the situation is important, and broadcasting can contribute to awareness. A congregation attempting seriously to utilize a series of broadcasts grappling hard with the basic issues of life may engage in self-examination leading to renewal.

Church membership groups can spend time wisely in seeing and hearing programs other than religious broadcasts. If Christians are to become aware of the potential influence of various programs on ourselves and on our families we must become more discriminating viewers and listeners. Group listening-viewing with discussion can help us in this respect.

It may be unusual for a woman's organization to tune together to a soap opera, but this can be a meaningful session—under perceptive leadership. Children in a released-time education class will be surprised that their program for the day is to begin with a Western or murder mystery, but it can become a significant learning experience. Young people, men, every group in a congregation can spend time together profitably in analyzing broadcasts and developing standards of judgment. Commercial announcements should come in for their share of attention. Families, more than any other group, have the opportunity to engage in such sessions, and parents can prepare for leadership by participating in similar activities in church organizations.

Not all discussion will take place immediately after exposure to a broadcast. Some of the more powerful programs will have an emotional impact which cannot be fully intellectualized immediately, if ever. After a period of reflection greater depths of meaning may become apparent, and references can be made in later sessions to programs seen or heard by the group.

The Search for Standards

For thoughtful response to broadcasts there must be standards of program evaluation. The search for these standards will be a stimulating enterprise, involving theological, ethical, psychological, and artistic questions. Professional critics can be helpful, but aside from a few major metropolitan daily newspapers there is little radio-television criticism in America and none even professes to take into account a Christian perspective. The most perceptive artistic criticism in Christian circles today is concentrated on the Broadway stage, seen by a comparative handful of people, most of whom already have certain standards of discrimination. The ubiquitous mass media, with an audience of less discriminating millions, are almost untouched by responsible Christian criticism.

In Europe the foundations for discrimination sometimes are laid in film guilds and clubs, some of them for young people. In contrast with fan clubs idolizing stars, these groups help viewers to refine their own judgment, to become more appreciative, selective, and critical. The same sensitivity directed to films is then applied to broadcasting. To assist this development there are special publications such as the *Evangelischer Filmbeobachter* (the Evangelical Film Observer), *Kirche und Film* (Church and Film), *Kirche und Rundfunk* (Church and Radio), and *Kirche und Fernsehen* (Church and Television) in Germany, *Kontaktorgaan van de Stichting Film Centrum* (Members' Bulletin of the Dutch Ecumenical Film Center in Holland, and *Film und Radio* in Switzerland.

There is no single formula for evaluating broadcasts. Certain questions, however, may expose ideas which can be pursued in discussion. What view of man is portrayed in the program? Is he a puppet, stereotype, nitwit, superman, or a complex but free individual capable of becoming a son of God? What are the prevailing standards of life? What values are portrayed in winning a jackpot, becoming a celebrity, escaping to the South Seas or struggling realistically within the conditions of human existence? Why did you laugh at certain persons and happenings? Did you feel superior to them or did you see certain weaknesses in yourself? Is the action in the broadcast contrived and artificial or believable and motivated? To which of the program's personalities are you attracted? Why? Which ones do you find repulsive? Why? And so it goes. Each group will discover avenues for exploration related to a particular program and a particular community. In the process listener-viewers should make discoveries not only about the program but about themselves.

One outcome of any serious attempt to develop discriminating habits of listening-viewing will be the recognition that the functions of the mass media extend beyond entertainment to enlightenment and inspiration. The churches can thus create and increase audiences for programs now suffering from lack of interest. In many areas churchmen will also want to support community-owned educational radio and television stations; in a few places churches or councils of churches will want to operate their own stations.

Channels for Candor

A related outcome will be the desire to communicate both appreciation and dissatisfaction to responsible broadcasters. Unfortunately, stations are not accustomed to hearing from churches unless a program has been objectionable. There should be channels through which station operators confer regularly with thoughtful listener-viewers. Christians in both industry and the audience can help to establish and maintain such channels.

Once a relationship of mutual understanding has been established, perplexing problems may be attacked within the framework of local conditions. In religious broadcasting, for example, there is a persistent question as to whether or not stations should sell time to churches. There can be no single answer which applies satisfactorily to all communities. As an aspect of their public-service responsibility stations can be expected to allocate sustaining time for religion, although the precise amount is unspecified. Whether or not additional time should be made available on a commercial basis to churches depends upon a number of factors, including the range of programs currently available, the quality of additional programs being proposed, and the financial condition of the station. It is conceivable, for example, that in a small community where the operation of a radio or television station is a marginal financial venture, the churches would have reason to pay their share of the expenses which make the broadcasting service possible.

The churches' main concern, however, will not be with a station's policies concerning religious broadcasting but with its over-all program schedule. This does not mean that the public will be telling a private owner how to run his business. It means that citizens will be taking an interest in the use of air waves which belong to them.

The nature of this advisory relationship will vary with the station and area. In some situations a committee may

represent listener-viewers; in others no such formal structure will be necessary. The more spontaneous and unsolic-
ited the comments, the more attention they are likely to
receive. Whatever the system, the station should receive
an audience response which is representative of the most
thoughtful and responsible elements in the community,
certainly including churchmen. When religious groups
demonstrate that they are conscious of the problems of
the media and eager to become better informed concerning them, the industry may glimpse the role which the
church could play in the world of radio-television.

Nationally, as noted earlier, there must be a clarification
of the authority of the Federal Communications Commission. If the Commission fails to assume more responsibility
for program standards than in recent years some sort of
citizens' advisory committee should be formed.

In all this the impression should not be given that only
a few unusually perceptive citizens see the need for certain improvements in broadcasting and that the executives
in the media are unanimously and unalterably opposed to
all changes. Many persons within the industry share the
disappointments and hopes of broadcasting's severest
critics. They often lack support, however, from colleagues
and from audiences, and the churches can help at crucial
points.

Persistence in the Pursuit

The pursuit of a plan for the church's ministry in the
world of radio-television will lead in many directions.
There must be an exploration of the relationship between
Christianity and the arts; there must be continuing research into purposes and programs, audiences and influences on them; utilization and discriminative analysis

of broadcasts must be undertaken by groups and individuals; there must be an intensified search for standards of program evaluation, and channels must be cleared for candid exchange of views with representatives of industry and government. If there is to be any sense of direction to this pursuit and if valuable resources are not to be dissipated in the process, there must be co-ordination of effort among as many churches as possible, locally and nationally.

The demands of this multiple approach will appear to be oppressive unless we recognize the extent of Christian responsibility toward the mass media. Broadcasting is a manifestation of the created universe and of man's God-given ability to unfold the secrets of that universe. The fact that radio and television also become a reflection of our culture makes it all the more important for them to partake of man's redemption along with his creation. As we look into the TV picture tube we find ourselves looking into a mirror and realize how badly we need a frame of reference from outside ourselves, transcending our culture. This the Christian finds in the good news that God in Christ has re-established lines of communication with estranged man and has called him to resume the pilgrimage for which he was intended, in the world but not of the world.

Christians have been slow to relate their convictions to the situation existing in broadcasting. The industry has been quick to see the possibilities of the media but reluctant to face the accompanying dangers. The church which should have been alert to both has recognized neither, with the result that there has been little genuine communication between two agencies supposedly engaged in communication.

In twentieth-century America broadcasting is a giant. It is not a monster although it could conceivably become one; it is more likely to degenerate into a buffoon and a hawker of wares. At times it is an ally of the church, at other times an enemy. The church will continue to be in contact with the giant at many times in many places. The resultant relationship can become a creative collaboration or a sparring coexistence. To try to avoid the giant is to run away from the sacrifices involved in reconciliation. To enter into any sort of meaningful relationship with him is to become engaged in a struggle which will try the soul.

Full-time workers on behalf of the church in the media know some of the qualifications needed for the struggle. They must have insight, patience, and courage: keen insight into theology, art, and communication theory; inexhaustible patience to deal with representatives of the church and industry; and reckless courage to risk their professional careers in a venture which is constantly in danger of being relegated to insignificance by industry or repudiated by the church. Under such conditions a Christian's sense of personal commitment will often be strained precariously.

This does not mean that the burden of the church's task in the world of radio-television can be delegated to church-employed broadcasting specialists. It must be shared by all Christians in broadcasting, by ministers, church executives, teachers, parents, and all listener-viewers.

Instead of a pat plan, then, we propose a pursuit which to some will seem hopelessly ethereal and complex. However, prospects for this pursuit need not be depressing. T. S. Eliot has referred to the idea of poetic drama as "an unattainable ideal," but he explains that this is why it interests him, for "it provides an incentive towards further experiment and exploration, beyond any goal which there is prospect of attaining."[8] The mature Christian understands the exhilaration of the quest for such an elusive goal. Eye hath not seen nor ear heard what is possible for the church in the world of radio-television if there is persistence in the pursuit.

Behind the Scenes on TV

A Who's Who of the Factors and Forces That Determine the Shape of the Picture on the Home Screen[1]

By JACK GOULD

The quiz show scandal and last week's running argument over how television should correct abuses has focused attention on the structure of commercial broadcasting.

The multitude of voices crying out to be heard reflects one of the contributing causes to television's current deluge of problems: the fantastic complexity of TV and the number and diversity of individuals which one way or another may influence what appears on the screen. What follows, accordingly, is an elementary primer on the organization of TV.

The Federal Communications Commission: This agency, established by Congress, has the job of doling out licenses to operate on the air. Its headache is that there are not enough available good channels to satisfy all who would like to use the air. As a result of this shortage, it must choose one applicant over another. Since in itself a license may be worth millions of dollars, the lobbying pressures upon the FCC have been fantastically severe. To all intents and purposes there has been illegal "trafficking" in licenses and the FCC itself has been touched by scandal. Moreover, the FCC is subject to rule by the Senate and House, many members of which have large or small personal investments in broadcasting stations.

The Individual Station: Under Federal law it is the owner of the individual station who in theory has the final responsibility for what is transmitted over his channel. Upon his shoulder supposedly rests the ultimate obligation to serve the public interest and, if he fails, it is nominally his license that is in jeopardy.

The make-up of the ownership of individual stations is extremely varied. In addition to Congressmen, for example, station owners in particular include many newspapers and nationally known magazines, some of which have been very harsh on TV's morals while simultaneously banking their share of the revenue from the now disgraced quizzes.

In actual practice the concept of individual station control has been little more than a legal fantasy. No station of itself could afford the cost of modern entertainment nor in technical isolation could it bring the visual wonders from afar into its own area. As a practical matter, therefore, all but a handful of TV stations in larger areas are affiliated with one or more of the three major networks—the American Broadcasting Company, the Columbia Broadcasting System or the National Broadcasting Company.

The Networks: The networks play not only the biggest role in TV but also the most varied. First, a network is a station owner. All three chains have control, total or partial, of individual stations in key cities. The stations actually may represent the larger portion of a network's revenue. Only through these stations does the FCC have any direct licensing power over a network.

But a network's primary and most publicized function is that of a program source. As a program source it assumes and is granted control over the programing carried by hundreds of stations throughout the nation. The network knows what is contained in a given specific program; the individual station seldom does.

Since practically all of the nation's programing funnels through the network offices in one way or another, the chains have been credited with both the medium's triumphs and its failings.

But one formidable dilemma of the networks is that while they are recognized as the primary source of TV fare, they cannot always control the balance in programing.

On the other hand, the extent of practical network control over programing varies from total to nil. With some programs the network is responsible from start to finish for the end result. With others, responsibility is shared in many different ways. With still others, the network is little more than a peddler of time.

The Advertising Agencies: The advertising agencies are the middlemen of TV; they are the liaison between the companies that pay the bills and the networks.

Advertising agencies function in a variety of manners. They may initiate ideas for shows in their own shop and then assign the actual production to others. Or they may pick up shows produced by others and decide to put them on the network.

The agency is a specialist in determining that a given show reach enough people to justify the advertising expenditure or serve the desired advertising objective. It is also the agency's responsibility to see that a show does not embarrass its client, i.e., the sponsor. The agency, as a result of close consultation with the advertising departments of sponsors, determines the volume, content and taste of commercials. By the power of its purse the agency exercises what in all other fields would be regarded as the dominant producing power; yet in television, advertising agencies rigidly adhere to a traditional policy of total anonymity.

Package Producers: The so-called "package producers" are essentially independent sources of programing, ranging from such firms as Goodson & Todman, foremost specialists in audience-participation programing, to the colossus of show business, the Music Corporation of America, or to the more individualistic entrepreneur such as David Susskind.

Package producers may come up with their own ideas and sell them directly either to a network, advertising agency or individual station. Part of their overhead is to prepare plans or even costly pilot films and then try to make a successful sale; the mortality rate in pilots is incredibly high and the losses in independent producing fairly staggering. Much of the best program-thinking originates with the independent producers; also most of the worst.

West Coast TV film producers have constantly complained —with such success that it is a major issue before the FCC and the Department of Justice—that they should have more access to the air, that the networks are a monopoly. Where the line is to be drawn between ethical responsibility and excessive economic dominance is a TV problem still to be thrashed out.

The Talent Agencies: The expansion of the talent agency, notably the Music Corporation of America, is one of the least explored areas in show business. MCA, for example, produces under a subsidiary corporate name a great many filmed TV shows. It also represents a vast list of the most highly marketable performers, from whom it receives a commission on

179

their fees or salaries. The representation of talent, a synonym for a very real control, can be a most formidable influence on what shows are done for which sponsor or network.

The Sponsors: The men who pay the final bills in television necessarily dictate the medium's present form; their patronage is bound to have a governing effect. But in TV, as earlier in radio, they have had to live with an element in advertising that does not exist in other media: the factor of association.

In TV the sponsor generally wishes to associate himself with the content of a program and also its personalities. If these elements are positive and constructive from a sales standpoint, he is delighted; if negative, he is the first to generate the indescribable panic that can permeate the entire inverted pyramid detailed above.

The sponsor's dilemma, on the other hand, is that he must live with his own peculiar gallery of critics: 1. His retail dealers. 2. His competitors who are waiting for a faulty move. 3. His stockholders. 4. His wife.

Viewed more broadly, the sponsor's role is to capitalize on the glamour, interest and stimulus of the show business but avoid all the pitfalls of that business. Accordingly, his is the usual position of the millionaire novice in the entertainment world: his ignorance is exceeded only by his influence.

But the much-abused sponsor also must be judged in another light. Whatever the frailties of commercial TV, the system must be placed in proper perspective against other conceivable alternatives. No non-commercial system abroad is without its share of dullness, poor quality and censorship problems.

The Common Pressure: All elements in the broadcasting industry are subject to a unifying pressure: the fantastic economic stakes that can turn on almost every decision at any point down the line. Television by itself is now a multi-billion dollar operation; the total interests of the sponsoring concerns simply defy estimate. The underlying goal of television frequently and altogether accurately has been described as the pursuit of ratings; yet, in fairness, this also could be defined in the non-television world as the headstrong pursuit of success.

This is why the strengths and weaknesses of the TV structure always will be fascinating; they are those of society in handy capsule form.

APPENDIX B

Members of the
Study Commission on the Role of Radio,
Television, and Films in Religion[2]

DR. WILBOUR E. SAUNDERS, Chairman of the Study Commission; President of Colgate-Rochester Theological Seminary

DR. THEODORE F. ADAMS, Minister of First Baptist Church, Richmond, Va.

DR. JOHN W. BACHMAN, Professor of Practical Theology, Union Theological Seminary, N. Y.

DR. DAVID W. BARRY, Executive Director of New York City Mission Society

ROME A. BETTS, Executive Director of American Heart Association

DR. EDGAR DALE, Professor of Education, Ohio State University

DR. EDWIN T. DAHLBERG, Minister of Delmar Baptist Church, St. Louis, Mo., and President of National Council of Churches.

DR. TRUMAN B. DOUGLASS, Executive Vice President, Board of Home Missions, Congregational Christian Churches

DR. WALTER B. EMERY, Professor in the Communication Arts College, Michigan State University

HERBERT E. EVANS, President of People's Broadcasting Corporation, Columbus, Ohio

BISHOP EUGENE M. FRANK, Bishop of the Missouri Area, The Methodist Church

DR. FRANKLIN CLARK FRY, President of The United Lutheran Church in America

DR. STANLEY R. HOPPER, Dean of the Graduate School, Drew University

DR. FRED HOSKINS, Minister and Secretary of the General Council, Congregational Christian Churches; Co-President of United Church of Christ

THOR JOHNSON, Symphony orchestra conductor

MISS DOROTHY MCCONNELL, Editor of *World Outlook,* a publication of The Methodist Church

SIG MICKELSON, President of News and Special Events, Columbia Broadcasting System, Inc.

BISHOP REUBEN H. MUELLER, Bishop of the West Central Area, The Evangelical United Brethren Church

DR. GEORGE EARLE OWEN, Executive Chairman of Central Departments, The United Christian Missionary Society, Christian Churches (Disciples of Christ)

RT. REV. JAMES A. PIKE, Bishop of California, Protestant Episcopal Church

DR. LISTON POPE, Dean of the Yale University Divinity School

DR. EDWIN H. RIAN, President of Jamestown College, Jamestown, N. D.

DR. JOSEPH SITTLER, Professor of Theology, Federated Theological Faculty, University of Chicago

SPYROS P. SKOURAS, President of Twentieth Century Fox

BISHOP B. JULIAN SMITH, Presiding Bishop of the First Episcopal District, Christian Methodist Episcopal Church

DR. DALLAS W. SMYTHE, Professor in the Institute of Communications Research, University of Illinois

DR. ROBERT W. SPIKE, General Secretary for Program, Board of Home Missions, Congregational Christian Churches

J. EDWARD SPROUL, Executive Secretary for Program and Research, National Council of the Young Men's Christian Associations

DR. MURRAY S. STEDMAN, JR., Director of Information, United Presbyterian Church in the U.S.A.

DAVIDSON TAYLOR, Director of the Arts Center Program, Columbia University

DR. GARDNER C. TAYLOR, Minister of the Concord Baptist Church of Christ, Brooklyn, N. Y.

BISHOP DONALD H. TIPPETT, Bishop of the San Francisco Area, The Methodist Church

MRS. THEODORE O. WEDEL, Vice President of the National Council of Churches

DR. D. CAMPBELL WYCKOFF, Professor of Christian Education, Princeton Theological Seminary

Consultants

JOSEPH T. KLAPPER, Consultant—Communications Research, Behavioral Research Service, Relations Services, General Electric Company

DR. HERBERT L. POTTLE, Secretary of Board of Information and Stewardship, The United Church of Canada

REV. KEITH WOOLLARD, Director of Radio and Television, The United Church of Canada

Secretary to the Study Commission

DR. R. H. EDWIN ESPY, Associate General Secretary, National Council of Churches

Staff Consultants

MISS LEILA ANDERSON, Assistant General Secretary for Program, National Council of Churches

DR. S. FRANKLIN MACK, Executive Director, Broadcasting and Film Commission, National Council of Churches

DR. LAURIS B. WHITMAN, Executive Director, Bureau of Research and Survey, National Council of Churches

JAMES W. WINE, Associate General Secretary for Public Interpretation, National Council of Churches

Notes by Chapters

Chapter 1

1. Marshall McLuhan, "A Historical Approach to the Media," in *Communication and the Communication Arts* (New York: Columbia University Press, 1955), p. 107.
2. See H. A. Innis, *Empire and Communication* (Oxford: Clarendon Press, 1950) and *The Bias of Communications* (Toronto: University of Toronto Press, 1951).
3. "Recommendation of the National Council of Churches for a Study Commission on the Role of Radio, Television, and Films in Religion," 1958.
4. *New York Times,* March 11, 1959.

Chapter 2

1. Harman Grisewood, "Christian Communication—Word and Image," in *Sound and Image* (Geneva: Department of Information, World Council of Churches, 1956), p. 22. By permission.

185

2. Joseph T. Klapper, "Research Indications of the Capabilities and Limitations of Mass Communication," address to the Study Commission of the NCCCUSA, 1958.

3. Dallas W. Smythe, "The Cultural Context of Religion and the Mass Media," essay for the Study Commission of the NCCCUSA, 1958, p. 2.

4. Herbert Hoover, in Fourth National Radio Conference, *Proceedings and Recommendations for Regulation of Radio* (Washington, D. C., November 9-11, 1925), p. 7.

5. 48 Stat. 1091; 47 U.S.C.A., Section 326.

6. From Walter B. Emery's book manuscript in production, *Broadcasting Regulations and Responsibilities* (East Lansing: Michigan State University Press, 1960). By permission of the author.

7. Hearings on H.R. 8301, 73rd Congress, p. 117.

8. Jack Gould, "Ominous Proposal: FCC Official Would Ignore Balanced Programing, etc.," in *New York Times,* Nov. 30, 1958, II, 13:1.

9. Paul F. Lazarsfeld and Robert K. Merton, "Mass Communication, Popular Taste and Organized Social Action," in Lyman Bryson, ed., *The Communication of Ideas* (New York: Harper & Brothers, 1948), pp. 95-118.

10. Leo Bogart, *The Age of Television* (New York: Frederick Ungar Publishing Co., 1956), p. 23. (There is now a second revised edition published in 1958). By permission.

11. Max Lerner, *America as a Civilization* (New York: Simon and Schuster, Inc., 1957), p. 835. By permission.

12. Llewellyn White, *The American Radio* (Chicago: University of Chicago Press, 1947), pp. 94, 96. Copyright 1947 by the University of Chicago.

13. Richard S. Salant, talk to the Rotary Club, St. Louis, Mo., June 26, 1958.

14. From "What Makes Howard Spin," by Howard Miller, in *Time,* April 29, 1957, 69:50. Used by permission.

15. David W. Barry, "The Relationship of the Church to the Mass Media," essay prepared for the Study Commission of the NCCCUSA, 1958.

16. Robert W. Sarnoff, address to the National Association of Educational Broadcasters, March 16, 1959, quoted in *NAEB Journal,* May, 1959, p. 7.

17. Sylvester L. Weaver, quoted in *New York Times,* April 11, 1957.

18. John P. Cunningham, in address reported in *New York Times,* November 3, 1957.
19. Donald H. McGannon, quoted in article by Marya Mannes, "The TV Pattern: Signs of Revolt," in *The Reporter,* May 2, 1957, p. 22.
20. Smythe, *op. cit.,* p. 6.
21. Cunningham, *op. cit.*

Chapter 3

1. Joseph Sittler, comments at TV consultation for United Lutheran Church in America, New York, December 17, 1958.
2. Charles J. Rolo, "The Metaphysics of Murder for the Millions," Bernard Rosenberg and David White, eds., *Mass Culture* (Glencoe, Ill.: The Free Press, 1957), p. 170. By permission of the author.
3. From *The Image Industries* by Rev. William Lynch, S.J., © 1959, Sheed & Ward, Inc., New York. By permission.
4. Malcolm Boyd, *Crisis in Communication* (New York: Doubleday & Company, Inc., 1957) and *Christ and Celebrity Gods* (Greenwich, Conn.: The Seabury Press, 1958).
5. Rosenberg and White, *op. cit.*
6. Quoted in *New York Times,* November 13, 1957.
7. Perrin Stryker, "Motivation Research," in *Fortune* Magazine, June, 1956, 103:144-232.
8. Leo Burnett, on program, "Ad World," over WOR-TV, New York, April 7, 1958.
9. August Heckscher, "What Are the Mass Media Doing to Our Culture?", address to the Study Commission of the NCCCUSA, 1958.
10. John Galbraith, *The Affluent Society* (Boston: Houghton Mifflin Company, 1958).
11. Wilbur Schramm, *Responsibility in Mass Communication* (New York: Harper & Brothers, 1957), pp. 166, 216. By permission.
12. From *But We Were Born Free,* by Elmer Davis, © 1954, used by special permission of the publishers, The Bobbs-Merrill Company, Inc. Page 175.
13. Gunnar Back, "The Local Bind," in *Saturday Review,* June 7, 1958, 41:26.
14. Edward R. Murrow, address to Radio and Television News Directors' Association, appearing under the title "A Broad-

caster Talks to His Colleagues," in *The Reporter,* November 13, 1958, pp. 32-36. By permission.

14a. *Ibid.*

15. Herbert Mitgang, quoted in "TV News Freedom Held Restricted," in *New York Times,* Apr. 17, 1958, 63:1.

16. Sig Mickelson, quoted in "C.B.S. Aide Admits TV Lacks Freedom," *New York Times,* May 24, 1958, 43:1.

17. Jack Gould, "Avoiding an Issue," *New York Times,* Nov. 17, 1957, II, 13:1.

18. *The Nation,* October 19, 1932, p. 341.

19. Richard Nixon, address to TV and Radio Executives Club of New York, quoted in *Variety,* October, 1957.

20. Ernest Van den Haag, "Of Happiness and Despair We Have No Measure," in Rosenberg and White, eds., *op. cit.,* p. 529. By permission of Harcourt, Brace and Company, copyright owners.

21. Charles Boyer, interviewed by Marie Torre, *New York Herald Tribune,* January 14, 1958.

22. Gilbert Seldes, *The Public Arts* (New York: Simon and Schuster, Inc., 1956), p. 231.

23. Walt Whitman, *Leaves of Grass* (London: Bogue, 1881), or (New York: Doubleday & Company, Inc., 1954).

24. Edgar Dale, "How to Evaluate the Mass Media," in *The Newsletter* (Bureau of Educational Research, Ohio State University, 1956). Vol. XXI, No. 8.

25. R. J. Garry and others, "Television for Children," *Journal of Education,* October, 1957, 140:1-35.

26. Seldes, *op. cit.,* p. 103.

27. Wilbur Schramm, *Responsibility in Mass Communication* (New York: Harper & Brothers, 1957), p. 299.

28. Arthur J. Brodbeck, interviewed by Bess Furman, *New York Times,* March 21, 1959.

29. D. Dumazedier, *Television and Rural Adult Education* (New York: UNESCO, 1956).

Chapter 4

1. Sir William Haley, "Moral Values in Broadcasting," address to British Council of Churches, November 2, 1948. Reprinted by BBC, p. 9. By permission.

2. Burton Paulu, *British Broadcasting: Radio and Television in the United Kingdom* (Minneapolis: University of Minnesota Press, 1956), p. 380.

3. Quincy Howe, "The Rise and Fall of the Radio Commentator," *Saturday Review,* October 26, 1957, p. 40.
4. Herbert Evans, personal letter to the author, July 1, 1959.
5. Murrow, *op. cit.,* p. 35.
6. Kenneth Bartlett, address to the Broadcasting and Film Commission of the NCCCUSA, February 17, 1959.
7. O. A. Ohmann, "Skyhooks" (With Special Implications for Monday Through Friday)," reprinted from *Harvard Business Review,* May-June, 1955. Used by permission.
8. Lerner, *op. cit.,* p. 767.
9. Heckscher, *op. cit.*
10. John Mason Brown, quoted by J. P. Shanley in "Mr. Brown Talks Television," *New York Times,* 1957. By permission of the *New York Times.*
11. Reported in *The Berkshire Eagle,* Pittsfield, Mass., 1959.
12. Commission on Freedom of the Press, *A Free and Responsible Press* (Chicago: University of Chicago Press, 1947), pp. 100-104.
13. Report, *Royal Commission on Broadcasting* (Ottawa: Edmund Cloutier, 1957), p. 144.
14. John Fischer, "The Editor's Easy Chair: TV and Its Critics," *Harper's* Magazine, July, 1959, pp. 10-14.

Chapter 5

1. "Report on Radio and TV Policy," submitted by the Board of Information and Stewardship to the Executive of the General Council of the United Church of Canada, 1959, p. 5.
2. David H. C. Read, *The Communication of the Gospel* (London: SCM Press, 1952), p. 18.
3. Joseph Sittler, "What Are the Mass Media Doing to Religion?", essay for the Study Commission of NCCCUSA, 1958, pp. 4-5.
4. Hendrik Kraemer, *The Communication of the Christian Faith* (Philadelphia: The Westminster Press, 1956), p. 30.
5. Paul Tillich, "Communicating the Gospel," in *Union Seminary Quarterly Review,* June, 1952 p. 11.
6. Gerald Kennedy, "A Whimper from the Sidelines," *National Council Outlook,* November 1956, p. 13.

Chapter 6

1. R. H. Edwin Espy, address to the Midwinter Meeting of the Congregational Christian Churches, Buck Hill Falls, Pa., February 4, 1959.

2. Announcement for "Church World News," radio program distributed by Department of Press, Radio and Television, The United Lutheran Church in America, Easter, 1959.

3. "Preaching or Indoctrination," *British Weekly*, January 31, 1957, p. 1. By permission.

4. S. Franklin Mack, comments at meeting of Study Commission of the NCCCUSA, New York, June 7, 1958.

5. From paper adopted by World Conference on Christian Broadcasting, Kronberg, Germany, May 1, 1957.

6. Joseph Sittler, comments at meeting of Study Commission of the NCCCUSA, New York, June 7, 1958.

7. From *The Communication of the Christian Faith* by Hendrik Kraemer. Copyright, 1957, by W. L. Jenkins, The Westminster Press. Used by permission. Page 60.

8. Fred L. Casmir, "A Telephone Survey of Religious Program Preferences Among Listeners and Viewers in Los Angeles," *Central States Speech Journal*, Fall, 1959.

9. R. J. E. Silvey, "The Audiences for Religious Broadcasts," in *Religion on the Air* (London: BBC, 1955), p. 7. By permission.

10. *Christianity and Broadcasting* (London: SCM Press, 1950), pp. 34, 35. By permission.

11. Stanley Hopper, comments at meeting of Study Commission of the NCCCUSA, New York, June 7, 1958.

12. Silvey, *op. cit.*, p. 8.

13. Huston Smith, *The Religions of Man* (New York: Harper & Brothers, 1958). By permission.

14. Ella F. Harlee, "They Learn the Bible on TV," *International Journal of Religious Education*, July-August, 1959, pp. 6, 7.

15. Everett C. Parker, David W. Barry, and Dallas W. Smythe, *The Television-Radio Audience and Religion* (New York: Harper & Brothers, 1955), p. 414.

16. Alan Walker, *The Whole Gospel for the Whole World* (Nashville: Abingdon Press, 1957), pp. 55, 56. Used by permission.

17. Parker, Barry, and Smythe, *op. cit.*, p. 398.

18. Harman Grisewood, *Broadcasting and Society* (London: SCM Press, 1949), p. 85. By permission.

19. R. H. W. Falconer, *Success and Failure of a Radio Mission* (London: SCM Press, 1951).

20. *Religious Broadcasts and the Public* (London: BBC, 1955), p. 23.

21. Parker, Barry, and Smythe, *op. cit.*, pp. 400, 411, 412.

Chapter 7

1. Consultation on Protestant Religious Broadcasting, Exhibits A and C, respectively, *Preamble* and *Code of Standards for Protestant Religious Broadcasts,* May 15, 1959.
2. Espy, *op. cit.*
3. "Broadcasting Policy Under National Council Auspices," adopted by Board of Managers, Broadcasting and Film Commission, NCCCUSA, March 5, 1957.
4. Reprinted from "Christianity, the Arts and the Mass Media," in *Christianity and Crisis,* A Christian Journal of Opinion, August 8, 1955, p. 105. By permission.
5. *Ibid.* By permission.
6. George W. Webber, "European Evangelism and the Church in America," *Christianity and Crisis,* November 10, 1958, pp. 155-158.
7. Daniel Jenkins, *The Protestant Ministry* (New York: Doubleday & Company, Inc., 1958), p. 90.
8. T. S. Eliot, *Poetry and Drama* (London: Faber and Faber, Limited, 1951), p. 33. The essay is now included in the volume *On Poetry and Poets.*

Appendix

1. This article from *The New York Times,* October 25, 1959, is reprinted here in its entirety by permission of its author, Jack Gould.
2. A high proportion of the Study Commission's members participated actively in the Commission's deliberations, but several members of the Commission were unable to be present in its meetings.